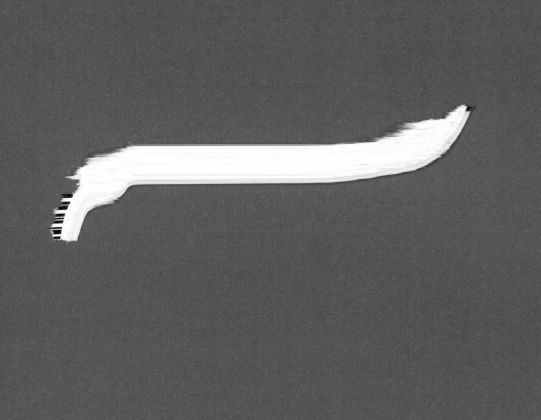

CHARLESTON
RENAISSANCE MAN

CHARLESTON RENAISSANCE MAN

THE ARCHITECTURAL LEGACY OF ALBERT SIMONS IN THE HOLY CITY

RALPH C. MULDROW
FOREWORD BY WITOLD RYBCZYNSKI

THE UNIVERSITY OF
SOUTH CAROLINA PRESS

© 2022 University of South Carolina

Published by the University of South Carolina Press
Columbia, South Carolina 29208

www.uscpress.com

Manufactured in Korea

31 30 29 28 27 26 25 24 23 22
10 9 8 7 6 5 4 3 2 1

Library of Congress Cataloging-in-Publication Data can be
found at http://catalog.loc.gov/.

ISBN: 978-1-64336-313-4 (hardcover)
ISBN: 978-1-64336-314-1 (ebook)

The David M. Schwarz Architects Charitable Foundation is
pleased to have helped make this book possible. Through his
efforts, Albert Simons helped Charlestonians see and value
the historic beauty of their city, and this new book helps bring
that to light. Additional support was provided by The Simons
Endowment at the College of Charleston and the Dean's
Excellence Award from the Office of Dean Valerie Morris,
College of Charleston.

To my father,

Charles Norment Muldrow Jr., PhD

CONTENTS

ILLUSTRATIONS

ACKNOWLEDGMENTS

I have worked on this book for some time and have acquired many kind words of encouragement and guidance. My wife, Anne, and children, Kristmar and Benjamin, have given me constant support and listening ears. My thanks especially go out to my colleagues Witold Rybczynski, Diane Johnson, Robert Stockton, David Gobel, and Simon Lewis. I am very grateful to the Simons family, including Theodora and Albert Simons III, Sallie Simons, George and Harriet (Simons) Williams, Serena (Simons) Leonhardt, Stoney and Jennie Simons, Richard Simons, and Sue Simons Wallace.

I also thank Ernest Blevins (grandson of Albert Simons's business partner Samuel Lapham), my Department of Art and Architectural History and the program in Historic Preservation and Community Planning, Diane Johnson, Mary Beth Heston, Grant Gilmore, Jason Coy, Richard John, Ray Huff, Jim Bowring, George Benson (former president of the College of Charleston), President Andrew Hsu, Dean Valerie Morris, Dean Edward Hart, Mary Jo Fairchild, Ashley Wilson, Diane Miller, Richard Wesley, Anne Fairfax and Richard Sammons of Fairfax & Sammons, Richard Cameron, Dennis Donahue, Bert Pruitt, David Cohen, Sandy Logan, Jim Thomas, Reggie Gibson, Robert Orr, Cynthia Jenkins, Shannon Hall, Clifford Zink, Roy Lewis, John Massengale, Macky Hill, Ted Stern, Katherine Saunders Pemberton, Cynthia Jenkins, Susan Sully, Craig Bennett, Charlton deSaussure, Jim Ward, Patrick McDonough, Mark Hewitt, Pat Mellon, Richard Marks, and Julianne Johnson (my graduate assistant who did yeoman's work to help bring this to fruition). Special thanks go out to Richard Brown and Ehren Foley of the University of South Carolina Press.

I have been fortunate to have met inspirational scholars in my areas of interest in preservation education and architectural history: Charles Peterson, James Marston Fitch, Joseph Rykwert, David De Long, Frank Matero, Henry Glassie, Robert A. M. Stern, Michael Graves, Jacque Robertson, Robert Venturi, Denise Scott Brown, Duncan Stroik, Robert

Adam, Sir John Summerson, Richard Guy Wilson, Henry Hope Reed, David Watkin, Alvin Holm, and John Blatteau.

I want to especially thank the awardees of the Albert Simons Medal of Excellence, all of whom have added insights regarding Albert Simons, including former Charleston mayor Joseph P. Riley Jr. (America's design mayor), Allan Greenberg, HRH the Prince of Wales, Andres Duany, Lizz Plater-Zyberk, John D. Milner, Peter Pennoyer, Thomas Gordon Smith, Richard Hampton Jenrette, Antoinette Lee, and Robert A. M. Stern.

FOREWORD
A QUIET CLASSICIST

The career of Albert Simons belongs to what Robert A. M. Stern has called the lost history of early twentieth-century American architecture. Stern was referring to the generation of traditionally inclined architects whose work did not fit the evolutionary model espoused by the historians of modernism.

The period between 1900 and 1930 saw not only the emergence of modernism but also the construction of some of a series of great classical civic monuments, libraries, museums, railroad stations, and government buildings that grace most American cities. The architects of these impressive buildings include such individual talents as Paul Philippe Cret, Charles Adams Platt, and Cass Gilbert, and prolific firms such as Carrère & Hastings, Delano & Aldrich and Warren & Wetmore. In the last two decades, useful monographs on the work of these architects have begun to fill in the blanks, and it is now possible to see a more complete picture of the range and richness of American architecture of this period.

Ralph Muldrow's well-researched book on Albert Simons is a valuable addition to this growing bookshelf. Simons was not quite in the same league as Cret and Platt, but he nevertheless deserves attention because he combined two important strands of the twentieth-century history of American architecture: classicism and historic preservation.

Albert Simons (1890–1980) was born in Charleston into an old established family. He was admitted to study architecture at the University of Pennsylvania, which, thanks to the presence of Paul Philippe Cret who ran the advanced design studio, was then the leading school in the country. After graduating, and during 1912 and 1913, Simons embarked on an architectural tour of France, Germany, Italy, Greece, and Turkey. In Paris, he briefly studied with Ernest Hébrard, an École des Beaux-Arts graduate, Prix de Rome winner, and the author of a definitive archaeological reconstruction of Diocletian's Palace in Split. Although Simons returned to Charleston, military service in the First World War interfered, and he did not open his own practice until 1920. His professional accomplishments during a long, 60-year career are described in detail by Muldrow in this monograph.

Several unusual traits stand out in Simons's career. Despite his Beaux-Arts education at Penn, and perhaps influenced by Hébrard's historical research, he began systematically documenting American colonial architecture and the buildings of the South Carolina Lowcountry. Simons wrote articles and several books on the subject, notably *The Early Architecture of Charleston*, which was published by the American Institute of Architects. He also taught at the College of Charleston, where he helped to establish a department of fine arts. He was interested in history and, long before it was fashionable, recovered architectural fragments from Charleston buildings facing demolition. "It distresses me painfully to see our fine old buildings torn down, and their contents wrecked," he wrote, "or what is more humiliating sold to aliens and shipped away to enrich some other community more appreciative of such things than ourselves." Many of the fragments he salvaged found their way to the Charleston Museum where they are safeguarded for posterity.

Simons's story is also the story of Charleston, a remarkable city. Muldrow weaves the two themes together, drawing a picture of the Charleston Renaissance of the 1910s and 1920s, in which Simons was an active participant. Much of his architectural practice involved renovating and enlarging old buildings, and out of this developed his unusual interest in historic preservation. Thanks in part to his activism, Charleston became the first American city to adopt local selective zoning for the purpose of historic preservation—an important first. In 1931, the city passed an ordinance creating the Charleston Old and Historic District in that part of the city known as the Battery. New construction and alterations within the district were overseen by a board of architectural review, and for the first forty-three years of its operation, Simons was the sole architect on the board, hence it is no exaggeration to say that he put his personal stamp on the face of his native city. Charleston's historic district became a model for the nation, and when larger cities such as Philadelphia, New Orleans, San Antonio, and Alexandria, Virginia, passed similar preservation legislation, it was often referred to as a "Charleston ordinance."

Simons was conservative in his architectural taste. This was perhaps the result of his extended experience in preserving buildings, or maybe it was just a reflection of the provincial milieu in which he practiced. Most of his work—respectable but unexceptional—falls into the mainstream of the Colonial Revival. There are two exceptions, both from the late 1930s: a gymnasium for the College of Charleston and the Memminger Auditorium. The latter's severe portico, obviously influenced by the stripped classicism of Cret's Federal Reserve building, suggest that Simons was keeping an eye on his old teacher.

Simons belongs to that generation of American architects whose careers coincided with the advent of modernism, and Muldrow describes how Simons dealt with the arrival of the new architecture, of which he remained skeptical. "I have no quarrels with modernists, in fact, I admit that what they are doing is almost inevitable in this age that is almost wholly scientific," Simons wrote. But he remained a traditionalist at heart noting, "Much modern work is extremely romantic, almost melodramatic in fact, but there is very little poetry of enchantment in any of it."

The history of architecture is like a great flotilla consisting of far-ranging frigates, speedy corvettes, great ships of the line, and slow but steady merchantmen. All have a role to play as the fleet sails forward. Albert Simons was one of the smaller vessels, yet, as Muldrow's affectionate investigation demonstrates, he played a significant role in raising the consciousness of his fellow citizens about the built environment, not only in Charleston but ultimately across the nation.

Witold Rybczynski
Philadelphia

INTRODUCTION

The spirit of antiquity—enshrined

In sumptuous buildings, vocal in sweet song,

In picture speaking with heroic tongue,

And with devout solemnities entwined—

Strikes to the seat of grace within the mind:

Hence forms that glide with swan-like ease along,

Hence motions, even amid the vulgar throng,

To an harmonious decency confined,

As if the streets were consecrated ground,

The city one vast temple, dedicate

To mutual respect in thought and deed.

   (WILLIAM WORDSWORTH, "Bruges")

No one has done more than you for the Charleston community, and your
work is deeply appreciated.

   (EMILY SANDERS, speaking about Albert Simons, February 4, 1974)

There is always much to do to improve the civic realm in the United
States; improvements, especially in the built environment, can always
be taken to yet another level. Architects are especially good as civic
leaders as their training provides a holistic way of seeing the present
conditions and imagining better ones for the future. The Charleston architect Albert Simons was extremely active in civic affairs in Charleston;
he should be an inspiration for architects everywhere to immerse themselves in such a productive way with the community around them.

   Unlike more splashy architects of his time, Albert Simons focused
on the Lowcountry region almost exclusively, and he mostly produced
understated yet fine designs in the traditional styles, mostly Colonial
Revival, often with Craftsman-style details. He designed many "background" buildings that still serve to create continuity with the buildings
of the more distant past without offering unnecessary competition to

the existing built environment. This, too, is an important lesson to be heeded by architects and preservationists now and in the future.

Simons played a key role in creating the first historic district in the United States, which became the model for hundreds of local historic districts across the country. His willingness to serve on and with many national and local committees and organizations makes him an exemplar for architects in the service of their hometown. His quiet designs were consonant with his humble desire to design buildings that fit in with the extraordinary historic urban fabric of the Carolina Lowcountry. Emerging, as he did, as the best-trained architect in Charleston at a time when there were very few architecture firms there, Simons nonetheless made the most of the wide variety of commissions he received and expended amazing energy in roles of civic leadership as a designer, staunch preservationist, and planning professional. Quite importantly, he saw the fields of architecture, preservation, planning, and art as inextricably linked—a point of view that will hopefully return in the future.

His training in Beaux-Arts methods gave him great facility with the design of simpler classical architecture in Charleston. He was ambivalent about the coming of modernism—he felt that it was inevitable that the scientific ethos of the twentieth century should produce such an architecture based on advances in building material technologies, but he lamented what he perceived as the deterioration of design. Thus his practice serves as a rejoinder to the galloping and too uninhibited forces of the modern movement in architectural design and education.

Other than a few years at the University of Pennsylvania, travel and study in Europe, and service in the two world wars, Simons spent the majority of his life in his birthplace of Charleston. He was an architect of great note in Charleston during most of the twentieth century, and he worked on the local, regional, and national levels in the preservation and planning fields. His legacies in the strongly related areas of design, preservation, and planning are still felt today. His Memminger Auditorium remains a grand building and still offers the best acoustics in town. Countless other buildings, designed during his sixty-year career, constitute a layer of "rightness" and seamless classical continuity that adds to the elegance of the city. This study endeavors to recount his life, spent pursuing the best that these fields could bring to his beloved Charleston. Simons serves as an inspiration for public engagement by architects and other professionals.

Later missives to friends are fortunately available in the papers of Albert Simons that add to the interesting aspects of his thoughts and projects that are illustrated in this book. Albert and Harriet Simons kept up a lively correspondence with the prominent cultural advocates John Mead Howells and his wife, Abby. Their letters consisted of personal news but also illuminating mentions of shared architectural thoughts.

Photograph of Tribune Tower, Chicago, ca. 1931.
Designed by John Mead Howells.
Library of Congress, Prints & Photographs Division.

John Mead Howells was the son of the famous American writer William Dean Howells (1837–1920). William Dean Howells's best-known novel was *The Rise of Silas Lapham*, a novel pertaining to a businessman with observations on American society. He was a long-time writer for the *Atlantic Monthly*, publishing such writers as Mark Twain and Henry James. Early on he was in contact with Emerson, Thoreau, Hawthorne, and Whitman. Unquestionably that background had a pronounced effect on William Dean Howells's son John as he was able to envision his field of architecture in a grand manner with confidence.

John Mead Howells was also the nephew of William Rutherford Mead of the architecture firm McKim, Mead & White, considered the finest architecture firm in America at the turn of the twentieth century. Howells had an outstanding career himself, including the designs of several high-rise buildings in Manhattan. His most famous buildings resulted from a collaboration with Raymond Hood. Working under the moniker of Howells & Hood, they collaborated on the designs for the Art Deco–style Daily News Building in New York City and the famous Gothic-style Tribune Tower in Chicago, among others. Howells and Hood won a very celebrated design competition to garner the commission to design the Tribune Tower.

In the 1920s Simons's own firm, Simons & Lapham, was busy with commissions for new houses and restorations, including thirteen houses in the elite neighborhood called Yeamans Hall. They also added a wing to the main building of the College of Charleston and consulted on the restoration of Charleston's famous Rainbow Row. During that decade, both partners in his firm taught at the College of Charleston. During the Great Depression the firm thrived on federally sponsored work, especially housing. Both partners worked extensively with the federally sponsored Historic American Buildings Survey. The firm worked on the renovation of the Planter's Hotel on Church Street into the Dock Street Theater, and Simons designed the Memminger Auditorium in the manner of Robert Mills and his mentor Paul Cret. The firm also designed new plantation-style houses and restored many others during that time.

In the years 1930 and 1931 Albert Simons was part of a blue-ribbon commission that helped Mayor Thomas Stoney pioneer the first historic district in America and the first Board of Architectural Review (BAR). These served as national models for preservation planning. More than 800 historic districts now protect the architectural patrimony of many cities and towns. Simons continued to serve on the BAR for many decades while managing a thriving architectural practice that included the design of Robert Mills Manor (an early public housing development), the Dock Street Theater on Church Street, the College of Charleston gymnasium, and additions to the college's Randolph Hall, along with countless houses, additions, and alterations throughout the Lowcountry.

Albert Simons was an important part of the era now known as the Charleston Renaissance, a period spanning roughly from the 1920s to the 1940s. During this time, Charleston had an impressive culmination of artists, writers, poets, composers, and singers, including Alice Ravenel Huger Smith, Alfred Hutty, Elizabeth O'Neill Verner, John Bennett, Anna Heyward Taylor, Josephine Pinckney, and DuBose Heyward. Other talents were also drawn to the city from elsewhere, including Childe Hassam, George Gershwin, Carl Sandburg, Robert Frost, and Gertrude Stein. Simons was a member of the Poetry Society and the Society for the Preservation of Spirituals, alongside serving many years on planning boards and playing a key role in the Society for the Preservation of Old Dwellings (forerunner of the Preservation Society of Charleston). Simons's watercolors and sketches reflect a rare time in his busy life when he was free to create fine freehand images. The year and a half of travel in Europe and studies at the Beaux-Arts School of architecture are included in part in this volume. His later architectural drawings are beautifully done also, notably his measured drawings as seen in his book *The Early Architecture of Charleston* (1927), created with Samuel Lapham. Simons also contributed mightily to *Plantations of the Carolina Low Country* (1938) and was one of the surveyors for the creation of the book *This Is Charleston* (1944).

While much of his work remains, even more was lost in the whorl of change in the physical environment of Charleston as he had to jettison many drawings each time he moved his office or home. I have attempted to glean the best from collections, architectural work, and memories from his family and friends. I have tried to meld those sources with the larger milieu in which he played such an important role, both in Charleston and nationally. He was pivotal in the preservation of Charleston while maintaining a gallant architectural practice in his own right along with a compelling interest in the artistic and literary movements in his hometown, "the City by the Sea."[1]

The work of Simons is relevant today as design for new classical and traditional buildings has come full cycle and is once again preferred by many. The clarity of the architectural character of Simons's oeuvre fits seamlessly into the traditional work that has come back into vogue with the still young twenty-first century. The design work of Simons, previously overshadowed by his great civic contributions, has its own lessons to teach designers, both today and far into the future.

ONE

FROM A CHARLESTON FAMILY

To Tell of the passing of nations,

Of the exquisite ruin of coasts,

Of the silvery change and the Flux of existence,

And of love that remakes us…

(Charleston Poet BEATRICE WITTE RAVENEL, 1870–1956)

Charlestonians built differently on the land. Tall, narrow houses with side yards make for a unique urbanism in a town noted for its great wealth and close connections with England and the Caribbean islands from the eighteenth century until the Civil War. The rhythm of the ubiquitous "single houses" infused the urban experience with trees and gardens. The continuous use of the shape and type of the single house for several centuries belies the existence of changing architectural styles, fires, hurricanes, a major earthquake, and wars. Into this persistent urban armature of large blocks with deep and narrow lots and long, narrow houses came people from myriad backgrounds. Geneticists say the historic area in Charleston has some of the longest records of known bloodlines in America, and that is something Charlestonians value greatly. The Simons family (pronounced like the more common name "Simmons") descends from one of the earliest settlers.

Albert Simons was the son of medical doctor Thomas Grange Simons and Serena Daniel (Aiken) Simons. He was born on July 6, 1890, to the great joy of his parents and was the youngest of seven children. It was a family joke that Albert wasn't given a middle name because they had run out of options![1]

Albert wrote the introduction to a book on the Simons family history and genealogy. An excerpt here reflects the admiration that Simons and his family had for Simons's father:

Photograph of Middleburg Plantation by Macky Hill, former owner.

[Thomas Grange Simons III] is a logical choice because this man as soldier, physician, and citizen was pre-eminently the expression of a familial society which had been maturing for six generations on American soil and had fully developed in him the qualities of self reliance and desire to serve the public weal…so many related families are woven into the warp and woof of this tapestry that it has become much more the chronicle of a group of families associated for many generations with the Lowcountry of South Carolina. It is hoped that this record will be of interest, not only for the many descendants of the early patriarchs and matriarchs listed herein, but to all students of early American life.

Indeed, the Simons family traces its history and name to Benjamin Simons I (1672–1717), a French Huguenot who was born in France in the region of New Rochelle and the Île de Ré on the Bay of Biscay. He was adopted by his aunt Martha DuPre, the wife of a Huguenot minister named Josias DuPre. Along with a great number of Huguenots, the DuPres fled France when King Louis XIV rescinded the Edict of Nantes, which had previously protected these French Protestants. The family initially went to the Netherlands, settling for a time in the town of Middleburg in the province of Zeeland, Walcheron Island. From there the family came to the South Carolina Lowcountry via England. Many Huguenots came to South Carolina seeking a new life because of the tolerant laws regarding diverse religions. These articles of incorporation for the Carolinas were

Etching of Dr. Thomas Grange Simons by Leila Waring.
Courtesy Special Collections at the College of Charleston.

written by one of the eight Lords Proprietor, Lord Ashley Cooper, and none less than his physician, the political philosopher John Locke.[2]

The family, which included Benjamin Simons, was in South Carolina by 1686, living in the Orange Quarter on the south bank of the East Branch of the Cooper River. Benjamin built a wood-frame house that he named Middleburg after the town the family had lived in in the Netherlands. The house dates to 1697 and stands today as one of the oldest frame houses in the South and certainly an important artifact of early American life. One hundred acres were allocated to Benjamin Simons in 1697, which increased through time to 2,599 acres at the death of

Benjamin Simons III in 1789. Like many Huguenots, the Simons family prospered greatly from the cultivation of the most important crop in the Lowcountry—rice. Historic letters show Simons and his progeny to be community leaders. Benjamin Simons II was a factor in downtown Charleston with a counting house at Adger's Wharf. Twentieth-century descendants include US Senator Burnett Maybank and the author Katherine Drayton Myrant Simons.

Thomas Grange Simons I (1789–1836) had a downtown house at 128 Bull Street and a plantation on nearby James Island called the Crescent. Thomas Grange Simons II (1818–1904) had nine children who were uncles and aunts to Albert Simons. Albert Simons's father, Thomas Grange Simons III, MD, LLD, was born in 1843 and lived until 1927. He entered the College of Charleston in 1860 for one year and left to join the Confederate Army as a member of the Washington Light Infantry. He was commended for bravery, having been wounded three times in battle. He completed studies in medicine after the war at the South Carolina Medical College and served in response to the yellow fever epidemics in 1871 and 1873, and he aided during outbreaks elsewhere. In Charleston he was a city councilman and a member of the faculty of the South Carolina Medical College. He served as the chairman of the South Carolina Board of Health and worked to improve national quarantine regulations. He was also responsible for modernizing the sewerage disposal system of the city and other epidemiological issues.

William Martin Aiken
Architect, Uncle, and Advocate

Albert Simons's study of architecture was aided significantly by the encouragement of his uncle William Martin Aiken (1855–1908). Aiken was from Charleston and graduated from the Massachusetts Institute of Technology (MIT) in 1879. MIT had the first major program of architectural study at an American university, and it emulated the process and rigor of the École des Beaux-Arts in Paris. William Martin Aiken worked for the great American nineteenth-century architect H. H. Richardson in Boston and went on to practice in Cincinnati from 1886 to 1895. He was the supervising architect for the Department of Treasury from 1895 to 1897 under the Cleveland administration and practiced in New York City from 1897 to 1908. Aiken created and oversaw a great deal of architecture work in various styles, including Richardsonian Romanesque and Beaux-Arts classicism.

One of the best-known buildings that Aiken designed was the grand Post Office building in Washington, DC, near the Capitol. Though he did little work in Charleston, he did design the cast iron bandstand in White

**Watercolor of a church interior by William Martin Aiken.
Courtesy Special Collections at the College of Charleston.**

Point Gardens on the Battery. He knew many nationally important architects and he may have been Albert Simons's inspiration to pursue architecture as a profession.

William Martin Aiken himself traveled extensively in the United States and in Europe, as was the prescribed custom for students in architecture school. This experience was formative for architects, allowing them to draw and sometimes measure the great monuments of the past; often these sketches were referred to later in the creation of new designs. William Martin Aiken was so adamant about the importance of such travel and study that he established a fund that provided for an eighteenth-month stint in Europe for Albert Simons after he graduated from the University of Pennsylvania in 1912.

Ink sketch of a Victorian house by William Martin Aiken.
Courtesy Special Collections at the College of Charleston.

William Martin Aiken watercolor of dome and tower.
Courtesy Special Collections at the College of Charleston.

Ink sketch of a Victorian house by William Martin Aiken.
Courtesy Special Collections at the College of Charleston.

William Martin Aiken designed the Old Post Office in Washington, DC.
Courtesy Special Collections at the College of Charleston.

Harriet Porcher
A Match Made in Charleston

Albert was to marry a woman who also was descended from old Charleston families, Harriet Porcher Stoney. Both of her parents were from Charleston families with long histories in the Lowcountry. Her mother was Louisa Cheves Smyth and her father was Samuel Gaillard Stoney Sr. Her brother, Samuel "Sam" Gaillard Stoney Jr., was an extraordinary historian of Lowcountry architecture and was often a collaborator with Albert on architecture studies of the region. The couple wed in 1917 and had four children together: Albert Simons Jr. (1918), Samuel Stoney Simons (1920), Serena Aiken (Simons) Leonhardt (1923), and Harriet Porcher Simons (1930), who married George Walton Williams.

Albert and Harriet were both extremely active in the artistic and political events in Charleston. She served in Civilian Defense from 1940 to 1945, the Charleston Civic Union (an organization for the reform of politics and improved race relations) from 1941 to 1943, and the South Carolina League of Women Voters (a strong progressive voice for improvement of conditions for the indigent, especially Black people in this condition), serving as president 1955. Harriett Simons also conducted research on the William Burrows House in Charleston (published by the Winterthur Portfolio) and on Charleston brickmaking alongside her husband.

Harriet Simons was a gracious member of polite society and a strong partner in the work of Albert Simons. She was a great admirer of architectural and natural beauty, providing Albert a like-minded, supportive companion for life. In a letter to Albert in 1917, Harriet says of Magnolia Plantation, "I love to go there with people who have never seen it before, and then when they stand struck absolutely adjectiveless by the wonder of the place I look on with the air of one who would say, 'yes, this is the way we raise things in South Carolina.' As for me though, I'm as speechless as I can never remember from one visit to the next just what a mass of glory the whole place is."[3] At their monument in Magnolia Cemetery, Albert gave deference to Harriet as the more important of the two, a typically humble stance that he maintained throughout his life.

Royal Atelier
489 - 5th Ave.
New York

Mrs Albert Simons

Harriet Simons. Courtesy South Carolina Historical Society.

TWO

MY LOST YOUTH, 1890-1905

"Remember now thy Creator in the days of thy youth, while the evil
days come not, nor the years draw nigh, when thou shalt say, 'I have no
pleasure in them.'"

(Ecclesiastes 12:1)

"Porgy lived in the golden age—Not the Golden Age of a remote and
legendary past; nor yet the chimerical era treasured by every man past
middle life, that never existed except in the heart of youth; but an age
when men, not yet old, were boys in an ancient, beautiful city that time
had forgotten before it destroyed."

(DUBOSE HEYWARD, *Porgy*, 1925)

The Lowcountry writer Josephine Pinckney recalls her husband remembering a church bulletin in which numerous individuals were listed as giving gifts as memorials. Albert Simons gave a gift "in memory of my lost youth," thus one imagines that he looked back longingly and sentimentally to his days growing up in Charleston.

In a letter much later, Simons describes a visit to the Charleston Museum and his observations there as a child:

On Saturdays, as a small boy, I used to go to the Natural History Museum which then occupied the top floor of the College of Charleston. I can remember standing at the top landing of the stair tower and looking down the open stair well to the basement where an elderly gentlemen was usually to be seen unpacking the most fascinating boxes that might turn out anything from a mummy to the vertebrae of a mastodon. Dr. Gabriel E. Manigault apparently did all the carpentry and taxidermy for the Museum as well as classifying and arranging its extensive collections and he also found time to lay the parquetry floor in his own drawing room...[1]

**Photo of Albert Simons as a teenager living on Montagu Street.
Courtesy Special Collections at the College of Charleston.**

Thus, not surprisingly, he had wide-ranging interests and was a very good student. He was born into a family that emphasized education and public service. And as was usual at the time, education focused on the classics with instruction in Greek and Latin.

Albert Simons was twelve years old when the City of Charleston hosted the South Carolina Inter-State and West Indian Exposition in 1902. Inspired no doubt by the World's Columbian Exposition of 1893 in Chicago, which featured huge, beautiful white classical buildings crafted by the greatest architects, sculptors, and artists of the day, the Charleston exposition was extensive, and the buildings were designed in a Beaux-Arts idiom leaning heavily toward Spanish Baroque. They were white buildings made mostly of "staff," an impermanent mixture of plaster of paris and straw. Other cities had followed suit, most notably

The Cotton Palace at the South Carolina Inter-State and West Indian Exposition, Charleston, 1902. Library of Congress, Prints & Photographs Division.

the 1895 Cotton States and International Exposition in Atlanta. Charleston civic leaders invited an architect from New York City, Bradford Gilbert, to design many wonderful Beaux-Arts-style white classical buildings on what is now Wagener Terrace and Hampton Park.

Gilbert's in-town associate for the project was Susan Pringle Frost, who was a leader of the suffragette movement in Charleston and was the

The grounds and buildings of the South Carolina Inter-State and West Indian
Exposition, Charleston, 1902. Library of Congress, Prints & Photographs Division.

founder of the first preservation organization in the country in 1921, the
Society for the Preservation of Old Dwellings (later the Preservation Society of Charleston). She was also a leader in preserving buildings from
a real estate perspective. A real estate agent herself, she understood the
role of economics, location, and procedures in achieving preservation
goals.

**Military parade passing in review before President Theodore Roosevelt,
South Carolina Inter-State and West Indian Exposition in 1902, Charleston,
South Carolina. Library of Congress, Prints & Photographs Division.**

Bradford Gilbert (1853–1911) had been the architect for the Atlanta exposition where he designed in the Beaux-Arts style. Gilbert lived in New York City, but he enjoyed Charleston greatly and bought a house there to live in part-time. He had designed the first curtain wall high-rise in New York City at 50 Broadway in 1889 (destroyed in 1914).

The Charleston exposition included an extravagant Cotton Palace, an art building and a Women's Building, among many others. It is hard to imagine that a young Albert Simons would not have thrilled to the rich classical architecture of that extraordinary exposition and the panoply of information therein. The city had hoped to align itself with the emerging concept of the "New South" with hopes that outside industries might move to Charleston and boost the economy. In the end, only a cigar factory joined the city, but it was a major employer—the American Cigar Company producing certified Cremo cigars.

While Charleston was the richest city per capita in the nation (enslaved people were not considered in this reckoning, except as the property of others, though they were in the majority in terms of population) in the later eighteenth century up until the Civil War. Though there is data supporting the sense of a long, inexorable downturn between 1800 and 1860, Charleston was nonetheless still the wealthiest city in American at the beginning of the Civil War.[2] It had not followed the powerful expansion of industry and commerce that the northern states experienced. Thus Charleston's urbanism was the reverse of the smokestack-croaked cities like New York, Boston, or Philadelphia, relying instead on agricultural products, especially rice, as the focus of commercial activity long after it had ceased to be the economic engine of earlier years. While factories in northern cities were in the downtown or nearby, Charleston just had a few rice mills scattered within the city limits and in far-flung rice fields. By the time that Simons was coming of age, rice cultivation had all but ceased,[3] and phosphate mining (which had been a fairly successful stopgap economic activity in the immediate postbellum years) had faded as well, overshadowed as it was by newer and better veins in other places. There was, however, a naval base established in what is now North Charleston that grew to be huge, along with some related companies such as the General Asbestos and Rubber Company.

Albert Simons attended the highly regarded Charleston High School from 1901 to 1905. In addition to being an outstanding student in Latin and Greek, he was also noted as the class cartoonist. His dry sense of humor was part and parcel of his personality. The High School of Charleston's motto was "Enter to learn, leave to serve." Simons certainly more than fulfilled those imperatives. Later missives to friends, preserved among his papers, add an interesting context to his thoughts. Below is one such letter that touches on Simons's early years.

Dear Abby,

My father left the College of Charleston during his freshman year when only eighteen to join the confederate Army and at the end of the War, in spite of badly impaired health, took up the study of medicine. Even with a large practice and devoted patients, our family lived in the most frugal manner as did everyone else in Charleston in those days. At school we were to be thoroughly assimilated along with Caesar's *Gallic Wars,* Cicero's Orations, and Virgil's *Aeneid,* all of which I found excessively dull but eventually I discovered that Latin could be the vehicle of gaiety and grace when we came to the *Odes of Horace,* a poet always singing the praises of ladies with such lovely names as Pyrrha, Lydia, Sabina, Leuconoe, Lalagen, etc.

All of this emphasis on the Classics had become quite outmoded in other parts of the country but continued here in Charleston because of our prolonged separation from the main stream of American life and the ensuing cultural lag that afflicted most of the South for an entire generation after "The War." It was not until World War I that the political, economic, social and cultural barriers began to disappear. As a student at the University of Pennsylvania in the early years of the century, because of my Charleston background I acquitted myself well enough in the humanities but was in a mental fog as far as science was concerned. In the post war years I became active in the affairs of the American Institute of Architects through the encouragement of William Emerson

of Boston and Clarence Zanzinger of Philadelphia and many others of
that generation who had studied in Paris at the Ecole and possessed all
the social poise and readiness of expression of the French and generous
friendliness and freedom from snobbishness which is so much a part of
our best American tradition. I know of few men of their quality today.
Just about this time you and John came to Yeamans Hall and, thanks
to your friendship, I was able to divest myself of any lingering sectional
prejudices that may have still clouded my outlook.[4]

THREE

COLLEGE OF CHARLESTON, PENN, AND PARIS, 1906-1913

Mensura vivimus
"By measure we live"
    (SIR EDWIN LUTYENS)

Aedes mores juraque curat
"She guards her buildings, manners and laws"
    (Charleston motto)

"Enter to learn, leave to serve"
    (High School of Charleston motto)

"Know thy self"
    (College of Charleston motto)

Leges sine moribus vanae
"Laws without morals are useless"
    (The University of Pennsylvania motto, Horace 3.24)

Having attended the excellent High School of Charleston and having excelled at the classical education in Greek and Latin, Albert Simons matriculated to the College of Charleston. It was a small but well-regarded college requiring Latin, Greek, and another language and continuing in a long tradition of outstanding education, including science and math components. The college is one of the oldest institutions of higher learning in the US, having been founded in 1770. Founding patriots included signers of the Declaration of Independence (Edward Rutledge, Arthur Middleton, and Thomas Heyward Jr.) and three signers of the US Constitution (John Rutledge, Charles Cotesworth Pinckney, and Charles Pinckney). It was also the first municipal college in the country. The

University of Pennsylvania architecture students in the studio in the 1920s.

College however didn't offer architecture as part of the curriculum, and that field was, to Albert, his most desired course of study.

Simons spent one year at the College of Charleston (1906–1907) before he moved to the architecture program at the University of Pennsylvania (Penn) in Philadelphia where they maintained an elite architecture school. It was a perfect time to be at Penn because the great French Beaux-Arts design professor Paul Cret had brought over from France a splendid and rigorous educational process. An elaborate school project by Albert Simons was featured in the book *The Study of Architectural Design* by University of Pennsylvania Professor John Harbeson.

After enrolling at the University of Pennsylvania in 1907, Simons graduated with a BS in Architecture in 1911 and completed an MS in architecture in 1912, under a University of Pennsylvania alumni fellowship. During the summer of 1910, Albert Simons was a draftsman for the Philadelphia firm of Evans, Warner & Bigger. Frederick C. Bigger, one of the firm's named partners, was pivotal in forging the profession of planning in the United States and in New Deal housing projects, both of which may have influenced Albert Simons's significant and later involvement in those pursuits.

Simons's personal design predilection harkened back to the architectural work of the nineteenth-century Charleston architect Robert Mills, especially his Fireproof Building and his First Baptist Church in

Watercolor wash by Albert Simons while at the University of Pennsylvania.
Courtesy of the South Carolina Historical Society.

A BVILDING FOR ENTERTAINMENTS

Elevation by Albert Simons while at the University of Pennsylvania.
Courtesy of the South Carolina Historical Society.

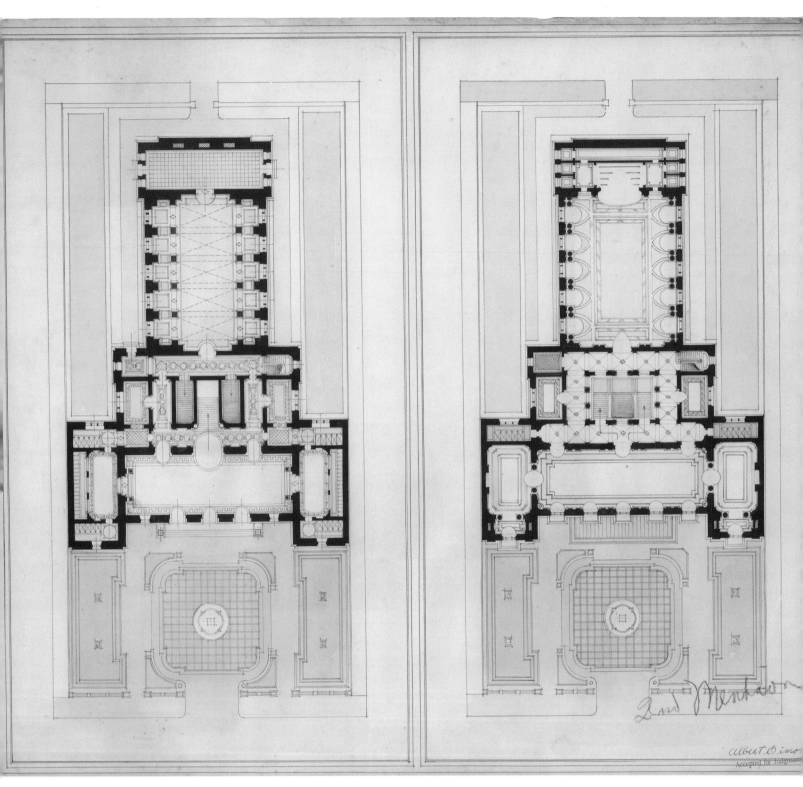

Student architectural project by Albert Simons while at the University of Pennsylvania.
Courtesy of the South Carolina Historical Society.

Wash rendering of an ancient vase by Albert Simons.
Courtesy of the South Carolina Historical Society.

Watercolor of S. Maria dei Miracoeli by Albert Simons.
Courtesy of the South Carolina Historical Society.

Watercolor of Alhambra by Albert Simons.
Courtesy of the South Carolina Historical Society.

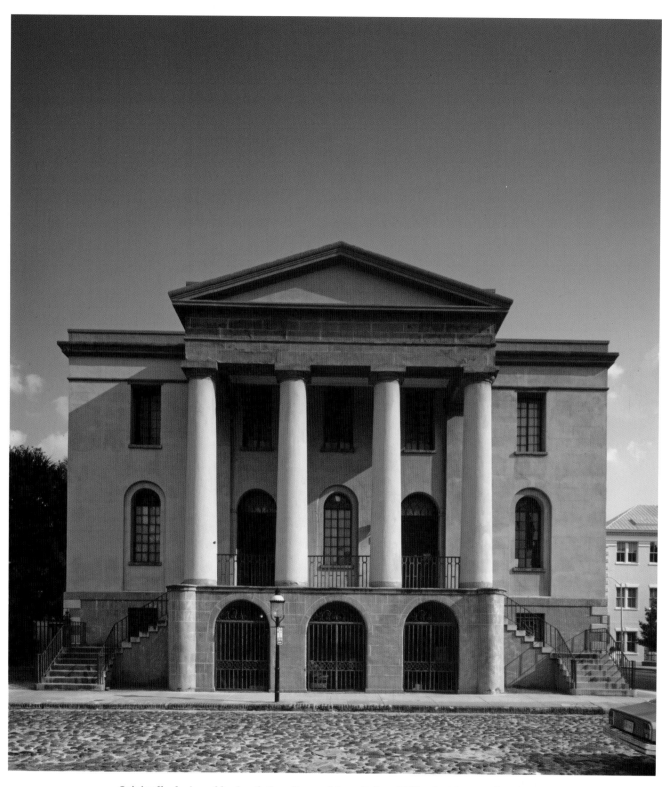

Originally designed by South Carolina architect Robert Mills, the Fireproof Building
provided inspiration for a young Albert Simons. Much later, he would have a hand
in its restoration during a significant renovation campaign in the early 1970s.
County Records Building (Fireproof Building), 100 Meeting Street, Charleston.
Historic American Buildings Survey, Library of Congress,
Prints & Photographs Division.

Charleston. The spare but well-considered proportions of Mills's classicism may be seen in Simons's own work at the Memminger Auditorium and the College of Charleston gymnasium. This reserved classicism was also a hallmark of the architectural designs of Paul Cret. Examples of Cret's work include the Pan-American Union Building and the Folger Shakespeare Library, both in Washington, DC.

Simons worked in Baltimore from 1913 to 1914 for architect Laurence Hall Fowler and the Roland Park Company where he designed exquisite historicist houses. The Roland Park neighborhood was laid out by a heroic pioneer of town and neighborhood planning, John Nolen of Cambridge, Massachusetts. John Nolen (1869–1937) was the first professional to declare himself a town and city planner. He helped start the planning profession in America and pursued beauty and congeniality in his communities, often based on the garden city movement from England. Roland Park was one of the most interesting and stunningly beautiful places designed by Nolen. Nolen attended the Girard College for orphans, the Wharton School of Business at Penn and the new landscape architects' program at Harvard. At Harvard Nolen studied with the sons of the founder of the landscape architecture field in America, Frederick Law Olmsted. This brush with Nolen's progressive design philosophy may have had an effect for the better for young Albert Simons.[1] At the same time, the firm he worked for in Baltimore fed his hunger for designing houses with an awareness of the colonial period in America.

Albert and Harriet Simons's close friends John Mead Howells and Abby Howells bought the John Stuart house (built 1772) in Charleston as a second home. They lived in Kittery Point, Maine, part of the year. While they had made trips to Charleston since the 1920s, they became better acquainted with Albert and Harriet when the Howells moved part-time to Yeamans Hall, where Albert had a great deal of design work. Beginning in the mid-1940s the Simonses and Howellses exchanged frequent and thoughtful missives. These letters provide glimpses into the profound, as well as the quotidian thoughts and activities of the two couples.

OCTOBER 17, 1947

Dear John (Mead Howells),

I read over your list of books with the greatest interest, especially because I was familiar with most of them and have quite a few of them in my own library.

The majority of these books are concerned with American Architecture and related arts, a subject that has come into its own following World War II. I can remember when I was a student at the University of Pennsylvania trying quite unsuccessfully to evoke an interest in Colonial Architecture in our professor of Architectural History and being properly snubbed for my pains. This worthy gentleman assumed that there was no Architecture worthy of his notice after the 16th century in any country and only the 15th century architecture of Florence was really worthwhile. Such a restricted point of view seems incredible today yet I suppose it was pretty general in the first decade of this century.[2]

Albert

In a much earlier letter, written in his senior year at the architecture school at Penn, Simons explained quite clearly his decision to study architecture:

The first point that needs explanation when an architect is bidden to give an account of himself is [the question] "Why are you an architect?" The answer in every individual case would be different, but in essence it would be that we had or were thought to have had artistic talent and that architecture seemed the noblest field in which to exploit this latent talent.

On entering the school with our minds thrilled with the works of art we are going to produce, we are considerably discouraged at finding no opportunities to display our talent. Moreover we meet with difficulties not reckoned on before the most formidable of which is that great Chimera with its three dreadful heads: descriptive geometry, shades and shadows, and perspective. It is good, however, that we meet our greatest discouragements at the outset, for they act as the test by which we may judge whether we have chosen the high course or not by what we are willing to overcome for it.

After the first year the work became gradually of increasing interest in spite of the fact that we found our talents are rather conspicuous by their absence when we are called upon to make use of them and it is only after laborious effort that they are trained and stimulated to any degree of usefulness. Gradually the memory stores up more and more material from which the imagination may draw. We find our work calling for greater and greater application and unless one is an enthusiast he will accomplish but little. In spite of the intense application he must be more than a mere soulless "grind." His work will have but little character unless he is himself a virile character. The men who produce the best work in the school are invariably prominent in student activities. As architecture is essentially a social phenomenon it is to be expected that the social environment in which we work will affect the results. Working as we do in large assemblies free from unnecessary discipline or restraint, too much value cannot be placed on the benefits derived from personal contact not only with the instructors but the fellow students and the stimulus to the imagination from talking to "men from across the seas.

After the four years are over all find that after all our knowledge of architecture is limited and that the problems we have worked upon are but a small percent of the problem we will have to [later] work on, but we have been shown the underlying principles upon which art is based and we have been taught how to think.

In this revealing narrative about his architectural schooling at Penn, Albert Simons reflected upon his experience as a successful student in a Beaux-Arts architecture program with some telling observations. He realized that the inherent value of the rigorous series of hypothetical projects was in the strengthening of a student's overall knowledge of design principles rather than extensive specific knowledge. Surprisingly, he pointed out that the general atmosphere in the open studio was one "free from unnecessary discipline or restraint." At the same time, he mentioned the mind-numbing difficulties of the work given to them in the early years, which undoubtedly were meant not only to build basic skills, but also to weed out students who lacked the requisite commitment to succeed in the difficult profession of architecture. He also mentioned that successful students participated in student activities, and Albert Simons himself was no exception. Among other activities, he acted in the musicals put on by the architecture club replete with professional-looking playbills and printed musical scores.

The actual architecture assignments were varied and interesting. These assignments were the typical hypothetical projects that started with small programs and worked their way up to larger projects, though Simons's senior year included some graphic design problems for the students to work out. Assignments included a monument to Thomas Edison, a building for a publishing company, and a school of chemistry. Similarly honorific on the scale of a building was the Society of Beaux-Arts Architects program for a memorial building by F. H. Bosworth Jr. Interior designs included a semi-detached music room for a city house and reception room for the president.

Another assignment typical of the program was a senior project designing an art gallery and library for a wealthy private client. It must have been vexing for Albert coming from Charleston with poverty surrounding grand vestiges of grandeur. The projects were accomplished in stages that were allotted a certain amount of time, starting with the parti (schematic design), which was a two-hour diagram that, when complete, was strictly adhered to for the duration of the project. Then an initial rendition of a more developed drawing was done in a specified time frame. This was called the esquisse. At last the rendu, or final drawing, would be made and rendered in watercolor or ink wash renderings.

Simons must have had a special interest in the brief for the American Academy in Rome competition, which was for a large navy yard on an island in the southern Pacific on a site that was to be one mile by one-and-a-half miles in size. The naval yard in Charleston was a recent phenomenon, which had breathed new economic life into a dormant city. This would have set a precedent for Simons's later work at the scale of urban design and planning, and he made explicit mention of this connection in his notes.

A brief for the Southern Intercollegiate Architectural Competition for 1915 called for a quintessential Beaux-Arts building type—a museum in a courtyard. The design was to be made during a six-week period, and the preliminary sketches completed in one day between 9 a.m. and 6 p.m.—en loge. The program dictated the courtyard was to emulate that of the cloistered courtyard at the Museo San Marco in Rome. This project reflected the city beautiful movement in its concern for the relationship of a public museum to public spaces in a city. "The building is located in a park and faces an important avenue. The formal elevation is towards the avenue, from which the building will be approached by a forecourt. The courtyard is to be treated with plantings and sculpture."[3] This holistic design approach included concerns of urban design, architectural design, and landscape architecture and planning as a unified endeavor that was typical of the Beaux-Arts approach to architectural design.

One senior year assignment at Penn was designing a title page for an architectural book. The direction notes that title pages of architectural treatises have traditionally been very carefully and beautifully detailed as part of architectural training. This project may have influenced Albert Simons in the graphic design of his bookplates and later on his Christmas card designs. He was also influenced by Philadelphia institutions such as the Philadelphia Sketch Club and artists of the Brandywine school, including N. C. Wyeth, Howard Pyle, and Maxfield Parrish. Simons exercised his design skills in another senior year assignment (November 1911), from Paul Cret himself, to create an ex libris (bookplate). One more graphic design-oriented project included in his papers is a memorial signpost and fountain.

While at Penn, Albert also joined in theatrical activities. The Sacred Cow was the 11th annual play presented by the Architectural Society of the University of Pennsylvania in 1911 and even came with a songbook of original vocal music. Other musicals included "The Discounters" from 1912 in which the opening chorus is "Architects, Architects," which begins, "In Par-ee now as artists we reside, artistic hobbies all of us bestride, our views on life we're willing to confide, oh, yes, . . . yes maybe we work and play . . . our ideal type is an architect . . . architects, architects, we've all felt the big call . . ."

Simons went on to travel in Europe with friends, with financial assistance from his uncle. They visited England, Italy, Austria, Greece, Turkey, Algeria, and Spain from 1912 to 1913. In 1913, Albert Simons joined the

Atelier Hébrard in Paris, which was connected his travels and allowed him a chance to study the great European works of art and architecture in person. Most of the experience of the école occurred in disparate ateliers, a private professional studio or workshop, where students would assist a studio master in return for critiques of their schoolwork. The students would be assigned hypothetical projects by the école and would then be required to work them up from a quick initial parti into the final rendu, with exceptional precision and beauty. It was incumbent upon a recent architecture school graduate to draw, study, and sometimes measure the great works of architecture as he traveled about, and Albert Simons created beautiful studies at many venues.

Many American architecture students of his day stayed in Paris for further study after their travels and enjoyed the expatriate community there. The first American trained at the École des Beaux-Arts in Paris was Richard Morris Hunt, who became a dominant force in American architecture. Architects who worked for Hunt went on to occupy influential positions in the American architecture schools, such as William Ware, founder of America's first architecture program at MIT and author of *The American Vignola*, an influential book on classical architectural design.

Undoubtedly, Simons was well-prepared by his instruction. Indeed, Paul Philippe Cret was the premier Beaux-Arts architect teaching in America. George Chappell, an architect and well-published architect, described Penn when Cret was there:

> Much has been written for and against the "Ecole des Beaux Arts" as an influence in American architecture, and many have been the discussions which have become wrangles as to whether this influence were precious or pernicious... There is one particular phase of this great school which seems to touch the inner spring of success... To the American student newly arrived, freshly graduated perhaps from a college, or technical school at home, what confusion is presented!... he is suddenly given what he has never had before-Liberty!
>
> Through back alleys and grimy courts some day or other he comes to harbor in the only social unit possible, an atelier. It is a feudal hole, usually, and he draws invidious comparisons with the comfortable classrooms of his schooldays, but it is his atelier with a strong spirit of its own, and in the long dingy room, over the battered tables and stools, he gradually learns the lesson of voluntary work... they are here working and they work hard and there is strife and emulation prompted only by honorable ambition.[4]

The students at the École des Beaux-Arts were expected to work at an atelier for little or no pay in order to learn from the master of the studio. They also received guidance on projects that were assigned by the

LE TOVR VISIG THE
CARCASSONNE

Albert Simons's travel sketch of Carcassonne, France (pencil).
Courtesy Special Collections at the College of Charleston.

Albert Simons's travel sketch of the Blue Mosque, Istanbul (pencil).
Courtesy Special Collections at the College of Charleston.

PILASTER CAP FROM
VIA-MERCVRIO POMPEII
from the notes of W A EDWARDS
ESq

Albert Simons's travel sketch of column details (pencil).
Courtesy Special Collections at the College of Charleston.

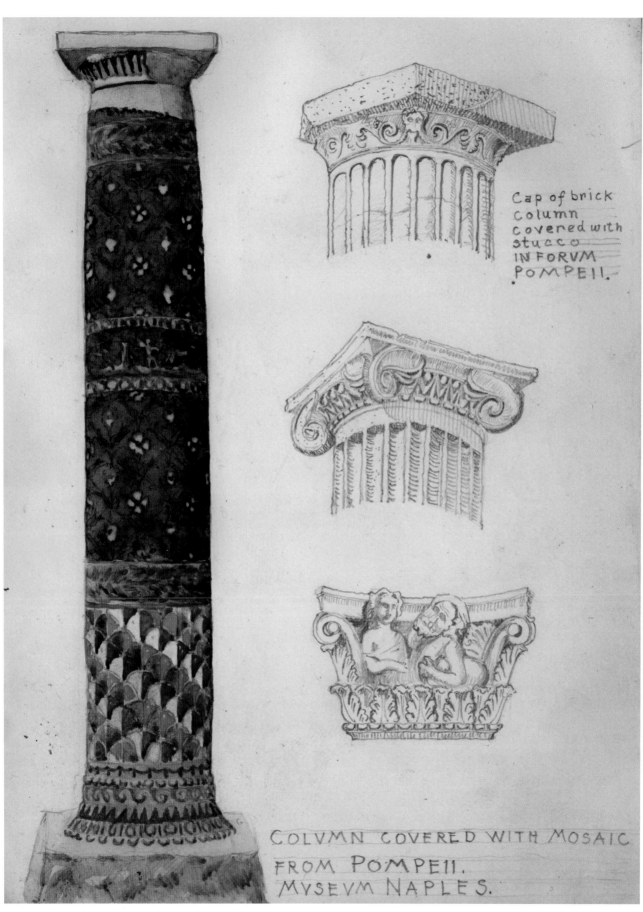

Cap of brick
column
covered with
stucco
IN FORVM
POMPEII.

COLVMN COVERED WITH MOSAIC
FROM POMPEII.
MVSEVM NAPLES.

Albert Simons's travel sketch of column and capitals (guache and pencil).
Courtesy Special Collections at the College of Charleston.

Albert Simons's travel sketch of niche and steps (watercolor).
Courtesy Special Collections at the College of Charleston.

JAN. 27TH
TEMPLE OF
CASTOR & POLLUX
ACRAGAS SICILY

Albert Simons's travel sketch of ruins at Agrigento (watercolor).
Courtesy Special Collections at the College of Charleston.

MOSQUE of SULTAN SELIM.
STAMBUL

Albert Simons's travel sketch of view of Istanbul (color pencil).
Courtesy Special Collections at the College of Charleston.

Albert Simons's travel sketch of the Château d'Amboise (watercolor).
Courtesy Special Collections at the College of Charleston.

CHENONCEAVX
2ᵈ OCT. '12

Albert Simons's travel sketch of a church in Amboise, France (watercolor).
Courtesy Special Collections at the College of Charleston.

Albert Simons's travel sketch of Azay-le-Rideau, France (watercolor).
Courtesy Special Collections at the College of Charleston.

Albert Simons's study of Chinese art (bamboo pen).
Courtesy Special Collections at the College of Charleston.

school. Chappell humorously describes the experience of a student from an atelier who joins the throng of other students at the school. They arrive en masse to be given an assignment:

There is a spirit of battle in the air for the rivalry between ateliers is strong but friendly and vents itself on those occasions in strident cries of greeting, exhortation or derision.... At exactly nine o'clock the doors are opened and in a wild rushing charge the cohorts sweep up the narrow stairs and spread out over their various floors to their favorite loges which are simply little stalls with room for two men to work in discomfort. After a moment the guardian appears to distribute the programs or printed statement of the new project and at the first glimpses of the blue uniform outraged liberty stands up on her hind legs and howls defiance. Through a storm of insults, jeers and stinging personalities, salty with wit, the symbol of authority wends his way, impassive and unheeding. "C'est la jeunesse!" He will observe philosophically and escape to his little office. Immediately there are more howls of rage, this time directed at that august imbecile, the professor of theory, who has dared to propose this idiotic program.

An Institute for the Preparation of a Therapeutic Serum." [a voice complained,] "one must supply lodgings for ten thousand guinea pigs!" "Ah, what luck!" screams a neighbor. "for I know how to draw a guinea pig in plan."

...at last comparative quiet is attained, boards are laid down, paper spread and the preparation of the esquisse or sketch is on. Friends stroll from one loge to another, discuss the parti, criticize one another's solution and return to their own places..." "...charrette! Charrette!" shouts a long-haired boy digging his pencil nervously into the Whatman [watercolor paper], and the cry is taken up from loge to loge and swells to a roar.[5]

Much later Albert Simons hoped for a revival of interest in traditional design:

I suppose that those of us, who were grown and supposedly educated when World War I broke out, were among the last products of the Beaux Arts, though this tradition did not fade out in education until the Depression or a bit later. The young radicals of the Depression Days are now gray haired conservatives designing most of the big jobs. The time should not be now far distant for a fresh crop of young radicals with hatchets sharpened to cut the props from under the established order. If I may venture a guess they will not lead us back to orthodoxy and Vignola, but I hope to a revived respect for those fundamental qualities such as scale, harmony and character that have always been in accord with sensitive human preferences and therefore differentiate Architecture from Engineering.[6]

FOUR

EARLY EXPERIENCE AND A WORLD WAR, 1914-1920

He is a polished gentleman of sterling qualities, well read, has traveled
a great deal, both in America and abroad and graduating as he has from
such an excellent school of Architecture at the University of Pennsylvania
is especially well equipped for his life's work.

(LUCIEN WHITE, about Albert Simons, 1915)

Albert Simons spent a year (1913–1914) in Baltimore, working for architect Laurence Hall Fowler of Baltimore and the Roland Park Company, which created an excellent early suburb in Baltimore utilizing evolving planning approaches and finely designed Colonial Revival architecture. The layout of Roland Park followed the curvilinear approach of neighborhoods being professionally designed by such well-known architects as Frederick Law Olmsted Jr. It was designed by the famous founder of urban planning in America, John Nolen of Philadelphia and Boston. Like many of these planned communities, it included a planned commercial area designed in a pleasing mix of revival styles. This experience undoubtedly influenced Simons later in his own Colonial Revival work in Charleston. Simons later recounted that it was the experience of working with Fowler and an architect named Howard Simms that bolstered his interest in early American architecture. He lamented that even the University of Pennsylvania with its Beaux-Arts approach had provided little enthusiasm for Colonial Revival designs.

Albert Simons returned to Charleston in 1914. As World War I caused a lack of regular work, Simons spent twelve months measuring and drawing old houses in Charleston as illustrations for *The Dwelling Houses of Charleston* by Alice Ravenel Huger Smith and her father, Daniel Elliott Huger Smith.

Per an interview with historian Gene Waddell in 1979, Simons recalled:

Albert Simons's travel sketch at Rennes, France (similar to depictions of Charleston)

None of the architects in Charleston had any work. I had been asked by an architect in Philadelphia to make drawings for him of any Charleston room that I chose. He collected drawings and he offered me $25 for one. I chose the drawing room of the Horry House (59 Meeting Street) because one of my cousins was living there at the time. Miss Smith saw the drawing and asked if I would do similar ones for the book she and her father were preparing.[12]

This experience was to serve him well for the rest of his career. The knowledge he gained of Charleston architecture, as well as the focused attention to the buildings and details by making measured drawings of them, culminated in a substantial and innovative contribution to the public awareness of the importance of the historic architecture of Charleston.

A Year at Clemson

Simons was hired by Clemson University to teach in their nascent architecture program alongside founding professor Rudolph Lee during the 1915 to 1916 academic year. Simons taught Architectural Design, Descriptive Geometry, Shades & Shadows, History of Architecture, and Appreciation of the Fine Arts for a small group of pioneering architecture students.

The fledgling program in architecture was conceived of as a Beaux-Art system, thus Simons's architectural design work in that vein was highly sought after. Assignments for the students were drawn from the type of assignments that Simons was familiar with from his own experience at the University of Pennsylvania as well as assignments from design competitions. Below is an example of a competition assignment:

A PROGRAM FOR THE SOUTHERN INTERCOLLEGIATE COMPETITION IN
ARCHITECTURE: A SETTLEMENT HOUSE

Site: A level site facing a street on the south and bounded on the north
and east by 16 foot intersecting alleys, and on the west by a private lot
which is nearly covered by a three-story tenement building. Upon the lot
across the alley to the east is a similar structure. In this congested district
of homes of the less well to do is an area set aside for the purpose of a
playground and as a site for a Settlement House.

The Clemson program differed from most Beaux-Arts programs of the
time, which were more grandiose in their focus. Simons's course instead
reflected the influence of the reform movement consciousness on his
nascent pedagogy. It also presaged Simons's later passion for public
housing and healthy accommodations for all citizens, a position his father would have advocated.

Albert Simons taught architectural history with a view toward understanding why a culture built in a particular way. In his opening lecture,
entitled "History of Architecture" or "The Architecture of History," he
noted, "Today we are the heirs of the ages and have access to all styles,
but we should strive to use them with discretion and only when they
accord with the character and purpose of the building."

Drawn Back to Charleston

Albert Simons returned to Charleston in 1916 and joined the architecture firm of Todd and Todd. He was almost immediately made a partner
in the firm, whose senior partner, A. W. Todd, had moved to Charleston
from Augusta, Georgia, around 1890 and had been one of the few practicing architects in the state for several decades. Todd played a leading
role in numerous attempts to create professional architectural associ-
ations in the state, a tradition which Albert Simons would later follow.
Simons noted that he was drawn back to Charleston by a particular project, the restoration and redesigning of the William Washington House at
8 South Battery, a grand house built by a cousin of George Washington.
He solved the problem of adding a modern bathroom to the colonial
building by putting unmovable shutters on the back part of the piazza,
thus stealthily enclosing the new addition. He also reoriented the house
toward the Battery. The owner was the prominent Charlestonian Julian
Mitchell.[3]

From 1917 to 1919, Albert Simons volunteered for military service
in World War I. In 1917 he was in the cavalry and was attached to the
Charleston Light Dragoons at Camp Sevier in Greenville. It was during
this service time that he somehow found time to marry Harriet Porcher

**William Washington House (Albert Simons's first commission),
general view from the southeast. Historic American Buildings Survey,
Library of Congress, Prints & Photographs Division.**

Stoney in 1917 at Camp Green in Charlotte, North Carolina. He was afterward attached to the French-speaking First Army Headquarters Regiment. He served military police duty in France at base ports and was then assigned to the Camouflage Corps (joined painters, sculptors, architects, and designers there, including Roy Charles Jones, who afterward headed the School of Architecture at the University of Minnesota, and Barry Faulkner, who became a well-known mural painter.)[4]

John Mead Howells, ca. 1923.

Friendship with the Howellses

John Mead Howells was a famous architect who was a good friend (along with his wife Abby) with Albert and Harriet for decades starting in the 1920s. The Howells family connections included his father, William Dean Howells, a famous writer, and an uncle, William Rutherford Mead, of the dominant architecture firm of McKim, Mead & White. John Mead Howells also did historic research and published books on American architecture, and sometimes its demise. Howells won the prestigious competition for the design of the Tribune Tower in downtown Chicago that was built in a creative gothic style. He also designed the Daily News Building and the Panhellenic Tower in New York City, as well as buildings at Yale, Harvard, and Columbia Universities.[5]

Howells designed Mark Twain's Italian villa, Stormfield, in Redding, Connecticut, and many other grand houses. He was the author of *Architectural Heritage of the Piscataqua, Architectural Heritage of the Merrimac* and *Lost Examples of Colonial Architecture.* Howells was interested in the preservation of buildings of the Colonial period and, after he retired, restored the Colonel Stuart House in Charleston as his winter home. Howells served on the National Fine Arts Commission in the administrations of Herbert Hoover and Franklin D. Roosevelt. He also contributed numerous articles on architecture to such magazines as *Harper's* and *The Century.* A graduate of Harvard in 1891, Howells studied architecture at the École des Beaux-Arts in Paris and began practicing in New York at the turn of the century. He was a fellow of the American

Institute of Architects; a member of the National Institute of Arts and Letters; former president of the Society of Architects diplomaed by the French government; a member of the French Legion of Honor, and an officer in the Order of the Belgian Crown.

Albert's long-running correspondence, especially with John and Abby Howells, allows us opportunities to discern unspoken aspects of Albert's thoughts. His various work after finishing his travels and studies was impressive. Before he had emerged from his twenties, Simons had already become a professor at Clemson, an illustrator for an important book, *The Dwelling Houses of Charleston*, a partner in the established firm of Todd, Simons and Todd and served in World War I. Simons had seen and learned a great deal, and as he entered his third decade of life he was embarking on a new endeavor—starting his own architectural firm of Simons & Lapham.

FIVE

WHEN "CHARLESTON" WAS A DANCE

A RENAISSANCE MAN IN THE CHARLESTON RENAISSANCE, 1921–1930

When I was younger

it was plain to me

I must make something of myself.

Older now

I walk back streets

admiring the houses of the very poor:

roof out of line with sides

the yards cluttered

with old chicken wire, ashes,

furniture gone wrong;

the fences and outhouses

built of barrel-staves

and parts of boxes, all,

if I am fortunate,

smeared a bluish green

that properly weathered

pleases me best of all colors.

No one

will believe this

of vast import to the nation.

(WILLIAM CARLOS WILLIAMS, "Pastoral," 1915)

The city is a "shrine for architects, artists, and others who appreciate its unique qualities…"

(ROSA MARKS, Charleston citizen, in a letter to the editor, later 1920s)

Like a romantic ruin in an English garden, the remains of Charleston comprised an extraordinary urban corpse after the Civil War. Charlestonian William Middleton wrote to his sister in Philadelphia that, "No one in the country in which you live has the slightest conception of the real condition of affairs here-of the utter topsy-turveying of all our institutions." Amidst the ravaged, aging rows of unsung single houses and privies and walls, as well as damage from the great fire of 1861 and the

Outdoor art sale near Cabbage Row. Gibbes Museum of Art

great earthquake of 1886, Charleston in the 1920s was a ghost of her former self. And yet, that was exactly her charm.

Bypassed by progress, labored by the weight of abandoned natural and Union damage, recalcitrant Charleston failed to attract northern investments in the same competitive manner with which other post-bellum southern cities flourished during the phenomenon called the New South. Savannah and even New Orleans fared better, not to mention the booming hub city of Atlanta. The new South movement was spurred on by journalists who called for southern places to emulate the industrialization and economic expansion that characterized the northern states. It also rolled out a red carpet for northerners to locate offices, factories, and any other would-be business in the southern states by promoting cheap labor rates, few unions, and warm climates.

While other historic southern cities looked toward northern investment for their economic revivification, Atlanta going so far as to create a monument to General Ulysses S. Grant, Charleston slumbered by the confluences of rivers, memories, and ideals. Just to the south, Savannah sported tall new high-rise buildings clothed in exuberant styles that were at once historicistically derived and creatively designed as that city moved to attract outside investors. All while Charleston's landscape remained largely unchanged.

Pencil drawing of the Miles Brewton House by Alice Ravenel Huger Smith

Rice Field. Watercolor by Alice Ravenel Huger Smith. Gibbes Museum of Art.

Etching of lower Meeting Street by Childe Hassam.
Collection of Dr. and Mrs. Bert Pruitt.

In The American Scene (1907), Henry James wrote about his 1905 visit to the remnant of the old South, "I could see it in the one case by the mere magic of the manner in which a small, scared, starved person of color, an elderly mulattress—just barely held open for me a door through which I felt I might have looked straight, far back into the past. The past, that of the vanquished order, was hanging on there behind her…so it seemed to me, had I been confronted, in Italy, under quite such a morning air and light, quite the same touch of a tepid, odorous medium, with the shallow crones who guard locked portals and the fallen power of provincial palazzini."

After the devastation of the Civil War, author Sidney Andrews described the war-torn city as:

> A city of ruins, of desolation, of vacant houses, of widowed women, of
> rotting wharves, of deserted warehouses, of weed-wild gardens, of miles
> of grass-grown streets, of acres of pitiful and voiceful barreness—that
> is Charleston.…We never again can have the Charleston of the decade
> previous to the war, because the beauty and pride of the city are as dead
> as the glories of Athens.

Flower Ladies by May Woodward (1877–1945). Collection of Dr. and Mrs. Bert Pruitt.

Architectural historian Kenneth Severens wrote, "After the war Charleston was faced with such a bitter economic struggle that there was no energy left in the people for the development of art in any form."[1]

And elsewhere he says:

> Charleston was a gentle town, far from prosperous and not yet recovered
> from ravages of the Civil War and Reconstruction. There was little
> money, no industry to speak of and the old saying, "Too poor to paint,
> too proud to whitewash" was a way of life. The old town seemed to
> slumber awash with sunlight, touched only by the soft sea winds. But
> it was far from a "sleeping beauty." Unheralded Charleston was under-
> going a cultural renaissance. There was a flowering of art, literature,
> drama and music. DuBose and Dorothy Heyward, John Bennett, William
> Hervey Allen Jr., and Josephine Pinckney were writing their books and
> plays. Alfred Hutty, Alice Ravenel Huger Smith, Minnie Mikell and
> Beth Verner were at work in their studios. Susan Frost began the work
> of Preservation. It was the beginning of the Poetry Society of South
> Carolina, the Footlight Players, and the Charleston Symphony. There
> was no free money from foundations or Government. What happened

**Actors Frank Farnum and Pauline Starke dancing "The Charleston," ca. 1925.
National Photo Company Collection, Library of Congress,
Prints & Photographs Division.**

was spontaneous, growing out of people's will to answer their own cultural needs; the lives of these creative people touched constantly. They enriched and encouraged each other. They gave the town a vitality and an identity which even the onslaught of "PROGRESS" failed to destroy.

The dance called the Charleston was almost a metaphor for the artistic energy of a revivified Charleston that learned to revel in its indigenous culture. The dance was derived from the Gullah culture that was and is a central part of Lowcountry heritage created mostly by enslaved people from West Africa. It caught on nationally through tourism and radio, capturing the freedom, exuberance, and prosperity of the decade after World War I and putting the semi-forgotten name of Charleston in the center of national entertainment.

The historic architecture with its patina of tumbled-down and aching buildings tinged with verdant gardens on their edges was adored by visitors from many places. And America thought of this outpost of mystery and southern charm as they shuffled and shook and danced "the Charleston." Alongside other southern cradles of popular music such as Nashville, New Orleans, and Memphis, Charleston contributed to the evolution of twentieth-century music in its own important way.

The dance itself grew out of the Jenkins Orphanage of Charleston which was founded in 1891 by Rev. Daniel Jenkins. Housed in the Old Marine Hospital that was designed by Robert Mills, a Charleston native who is often considered the first truly American architect, the orphanage took in Black children for shelter and food but also teaching and especially training in music. The orphanage band became famous for its jazz and ragtime music and traveled widely to raise money through its rousing music. So strangely enough, the staid and formality-oriented city of Charleston was a major player in the spread of a creolized American musical invention that could popularize its music as never before with the advent of the phonograph and the radio.

The steps have been traced to a traditional African dance called the Juba where two dancers would face off in a circle of spectators who would clap, stamp, and slap their thighs in time to a rhythm. The dancers in the center would compete against each other, performing increasingly more intricate and difficult steps while bystanders watched and cheered. There are certain basic steps that are commonly recognized, but the dance relies heavily on the improvisation, innovation, and individuality of the dancer.[2] Graduates of the Jenkins Orphanage Band went on to play with numerous outstanding groups and musicians, including Count Basie and Duke Ellington.

Alongside the dance phenomenon, there is also some claim to Charleston having invented the cocktail party. Local lore says that its late-afternoon timing reflected the Charleston proclivity to have an easy time of throwing a party after the help had left. In spite of Prohibition, there seems to have been a culture of private parties serving hard drinks; in fact, the renowned architect and preservationist Charles Peterson, who created the Historic American Buildings Survey (HABS) architectural recordation program, recalled Albert Simons giving him a recipe for a potent planter's punch from the Prohibition era. One can only imagine a golden hour cocktail party with members of the Charleston Renaissance gathered to update each other on their creative endeavors. Perhaps some of the following notable individuals shared their progress.

Josephine Pinckney, Writer and Preservationist

In her 1945 book, *Three O'Clock Dinner*, Josephine Pinckney recounts the tenacious adherence to customs from the former aristocratic strata of Charleston society. One custom still adhered to was having the big meal of the day at 3:00 p.m. with special locations on the long table for the different preferred foods; ham at one end, turkey at the other, with other dishes and condiments in between. Such customs were dying out but were steadfastly adhered by Simons's generation even after World War II and still by some in the present day.

Josephine Pinckney was an outstanding literary figure who was an important presence in national publishing, including poems and books

Ironwork overthrow of a gate designed for Josephine Pinckney by Albert Simons

that captured the waning but present set of behaviors from "Old Charleston." She was also a civic leader and an ardent preservationist. Simons designed an iron gate for her Chalmers Street home that created a very clever mirror-imaged motifs that together formed her initials "JP."

According to novelist, poet, and professor James Kibler:

Pinckney played a key role in the literary revival that swept through the South after World War I. She worked closely with DuBose Heyward, Hervey Allen, and John Bennett in founding the Poetry Society of South Carolina in 1920. During the following decade, Pinckney emerged as a poet of national reputation when her work, often evocative eulogies to a vanishing way of southern life, appeared in influential journals such as the *Saturday Review of Literature and Poetry,* as well as in numerous

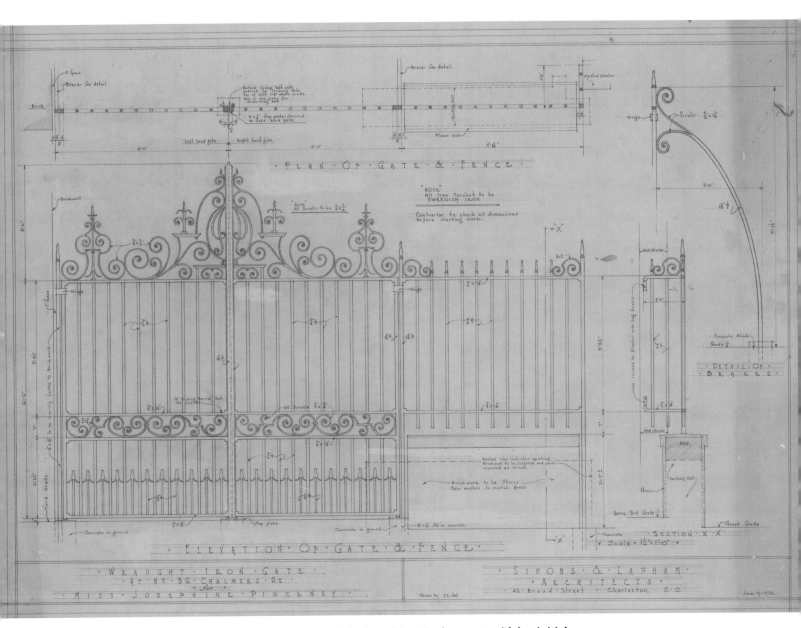

**Drawing by Albert Simons of the Josephine Pinckney gate with her initials.
Courtesy of the South Carolina Historical Society.**

anthologies. Her only book of poems, *Sea-Drinking Cities* (1927), received praise from Donald Davidson for "a luxuriance of phrase, a quiet humor controlling deep emotion.

Pinckney was influential in many social and artistic circles that included Albert Simons. They were comrades in arms for saving buildings and furthering civic progress while retaining all that was special about Charleston. She was recognized nationally by the American Scenic and Historic Preservation Society for the tactful manner in which she persuasively, firmly, and wisely helped to restore the city's neighborhoods and notable buildings. The support for preservation as an integral part of the cultural milieu of Charleston made for an especially dynamic and innovative atmosphere that is still somewhat intact today.

Etching by Alfred Hutty, *Bedon's Alley*, 1921.
Collection of Dr. and Mrs. Bert Pruitt.

Alfred Hutty Arrives to Find Heaven!

Alfred Hutty (1877–1954) is another case study in the cultural cachet of the Charleston Renaissance. Hutty was a gifted artist arriving in Charleston via the Midwest and North. He was invited to Charleston to establish an art school for the Carolina Art Association. Upon his arrival in 1920 he immediately wrote to his wife, "Come quickly, have found heaven!"[3]

Alfred Hutty from New York became an important contributor to the Charleston Renaissance. Having studied with nationally important artists in the Midwest, New York City and the Woodstock Art Colony in upstate New York, he came with training molded by graduates of the École des Beaux-Arts and excellent teachers of representational art. His artistic style accentuated the subjects that he depicted, so that his realism was merged with the sense that a poignant moment had been frozen and distilled with a fine, masterful hand.[4]

He directed the school of the Carolina Art Association from 1920

Photo by Albert Simons of Charleston alley.
Courtesy South Carolina Historical Society.

to 1924, at the Gibbes Museum of Art in the center of Charleston. His own work featured images of stucco building surfaces in disrepair and stooped figures relaxing in doorways. One of his most renowned works is Cabbage Row, a drypoint illustrating the tenement immortalized by DuBose Heyward in his novel *Porgy*. Hutty and Heyward were good friends who were brought together by the ether of the Charleston Renaissance. In his drawings, Hutty depicted the types of people that Heyward depicted in his writings. They both drew their inspiration from real-life Charleston models.

One of Hutty's major interests was Charleston theater, which had begun its long history in the building of the first Dock Street Theater in 1763. It was through his love of theater and his term as president of the Footlight Players that Hutty came to know Albert Simons. Simons had the commission to restore the former Planter's Hotel and fill the courtyard in the middle with a theater that reflected the early date of the creation of the theater troup elsewhere in the city. He traveled throughout

Photo by Albert Simons of derelict doorway.
Courtesy South Carolina Historical Society.

England to gather information on ca. 1700 theaters to allow the new design to have an appropriately authentic appearance.

Hutty was not alone in loving what he found in Charleston. In the Roaring Twenties, Charleston came in to its own with a surge of tourists, especially from the North, who came to admire the weathered but historic architecture, faded glories of a time long past. There had certainly been a heritage tourism component to the Charleston economy going back many years. Magnolia Plantation, for example, created a spur off the main north-south rail line from New York City to Florida for the convenience of tourists in 1870.

Portrait of Aaron Douglas, 1930, by Edwin Harleston
(American, 1882–1931). Oil on canvas, 32¼ x 28¼ inches.
Image courtesy of Gibbes Museum of Art / Carolina Art Association.

DuBose Heyward

Born in 1885, to an old Charleston family, DuBose Heyward lived in poverty. At the age of seventeen he found himself working on the waterfront to help his mother support their family after his father's death. While working there he observed the African American people and came to admire their culture. He began his writing career with poems and one-act plays. His most famous work was *Porgy*, which was published as a novel published in 1913. It was set on Catfish Row, a fictional Charleston tenement street. In the novel Heyward effectively used the Gullah dialect that many of the Black Charlestonians spoke.

Heyward and his wife, Dorothy, wrote a dramatization of the novel called *Porgy and Bess*. It was produced as a stage production in New York City in 1927. With the help of George Gershwin the play was made into a folk opera in 1935. It was performed often in New York City in the following decades, but only somewhat recently in Charleston, due to strained racial relationships.

John Bennett Finds Heaven

A central figure to the Charleston Renaissance and its progeny, John Bennett (1865–1956) was a writer from Chillicothe, Ohio, who moved to Charleston in 1898 upon doctor's orders to find a relatively warm place to spend the winter. He stayed for the rest of his life and had a successful writing career that featured a book, *Doctor to the Dead*, and a popular children's book prior to arriving in Charleston called *Master Skylark*. He was very involved with the cultural blossoming of Charleston's arts community; in fact, he was usually in the inner circle of cultural organizations. According to Harlan Greene's book on Bennett:

> For periodic relief, he [Bennett] turned to his first love, drawing. Along with local artist Alice Ravenel Huger Smith, Bennett served as an art critic for classes at the Carolina Art Association taught by Susan's [Susan Smyth] nephew Albert Simons who was quickly becoming a nationally known architect and one of the main preservationists of the city. For the first time there was a life-drawing class similar to the ones Bennett had taken at the New York Art Students' League.[5]

As mentioned previously, Alice Ravenel Huger Smith had hired a young Albert Simons to do the beautifully drafted and designed illustrations for her book, *The Dwelling Houses of Charleston*, and she continued to create extraordinary drawings and watercolors reflecting the Lowcountry. She was central to the artistic foment of the Charleston Renaissance as were Elizabeth O'Neill Verner, William Hervey Allen Jr., Anna Heyward Taylor, Anna Heyward Huntington, and numerous others.

Preservation Culture between the Wars

> "It might not be an exaggeration to say that the whole historic district of Charleston emerged as a grand design from the drawing board of Albert Simons."
>
> (CHARLES HOSMER, *Presence of the Past,* 1965)

While Simons participated widely in the organizations that were fueling a lively infusion of the arts in Charleston in the 1920s, including excellent traditional design work, Simons's greatest impact was in historic preservation. This is not surprising because the pursuit was so closely connected with the arts movements in that the imagery and content for most organizations of the Charleston Renaissance was based on the grand yet crumbling architecture that was so central to Charleston's charm. Charles Hosmer's *Preservation Comes of Age* covers the rise of the historic preservation movement in the United States. In the introduction and the acknowledgments, he credits Albert Simons, Helen

McCormack of the South Carolina Historical Society, Frances Edmunds of the Historic Charleston Foundation, and Mary Anderson for his information on Charleston. Hosmer paints the beginnings of organized preservation with a broad brush initially:

> Few people before World War I had appreciated enough the signs of
> continuous growth that formed the urban landscape to try to save
> them. Cities were considered wicked; in fact, many literary and artistic
> themes revolved around the country boy and girl who was ruined by the
> decision to move to town. By the second decade of the twentieth century
> this feeling was on the wane, and there were some preservation pioneers
> who saw real beauty in their cities and chose not to flee to the suburbs…
> it is no surprise that several early preservation efforts developed in the
> relatively stagnate economy of the South in the 1920's and 1930's.

A gap in the dismal economic morass in the South especially affected the rural areas around Charleston. Northern "snowbirds" saw great opportunities in buying entire islands and large tracts of land where they could restore the decrepit plantation buildings and make for themselves places to visit when their northern cities became filled with ice and snow. They had names like Rockefeller, Vanderbilt, Guggenheim, Kennedy, Baruch, and so forth. The firm of Simons & Lapham was the architect of choice to restore deteriorating plantations, often retrofitting them to serve as hunting lodges.

In an essay about searching for a southern identity, C. Vann Woodward comments on the impact of the "bulldozer revolution" on the sense of tradition and identity that the old South maintained up until the 1930s. "In the seaports of the South the antebellum years took on the aura of a golden age for the white children of the Reconstruction era. So it was understandable that the strongest desire to save the symbols of a forgotten past would surface in southern towns. The emphasis was nostalgic and centered on beautiful homes. This was distinctly different from the current emphasis on buildings of all types."[6]

In her book *The Making of Historic Charleston: A Golden Haze of Memory*, Stephanie Yuhl recounts the living myth of a continuity with the antebellum past.[7] But that past is a selective past that is gilded with proprieties they assumed were an extension of an idealized time of economic prosperity and when formality was the cultural norm (dancing the Charleston not withstanding). These trappings were diminished after World War II, but not entirely. Charleston still has the longest traceable bloodlines of any American city, and there are still family homes that are handed down from each generation while the national average of home ownership is currently approximately five years. The romanticism of Charleston has an analogy in the realm of architecture, and indeed in Simons's own work. His endeavors to create the Charleston

Old and Historic District and the BAR; his in-depth study of the historic Carolina Lowcountry architecture; and his new building designs seamlessly fitting into the built fabric of Charleston were all in service to the mythology of Charleston.

Certainly Charleston was a talisman for the preservation movement in America. The first preservation organization in America was created and run from Charleston—it was the Mount Vernon Ladies Association founded (1853) and led by Ann Pamela Cunningham. The first community-based preservation organization began in 1920 as the Society for the Preservation of Old Dwellings, formed by thirty active and distinguished Charleston citizens. Susan Pringle Frost, who had worked with Bradford Gilbert on the 1902 exposition, convened the meeting and was asked to be the president. Frost lived in the finest Georgian house in town, the Miles Brewton House, and she worked in the real estate field. She felt that donors should buy threatened historic houses and the Joseph Manigault house was a case in point. Mr. and Mrs. Ernest Pringle bought the Manigault house to save it. But bills ran up quickly and they sold a portion of the lot to the Standard Oil Company for a filling station. It seemed oddly comical that the beautiful round entry temple-form structure became the men's and women's rooms for the filling station, and that a tour of the house was offered with every tank of gasoline.

Albert Simons was involved in all of these efforts and more. For example, he was involved with the American Institute of Architects (AIA) and was asked by their national office, located in the Octagon house in Washington, DC, to create a book on the architecture of the Carolina Lowcountry. The national board decided to commission a series of books on the architecture of historic towns. In the prosperous 1920s the project sounded splendid; they asked Albert Simons to do the first volume on Charleston. It turned out to be the only book in the series to be completed as the Great Depression halted further volumes in the Octagon Library series.

The Octagon Library book of 1927 on Charleston was a nationally acclaimed study of the city, published during the decade when the city was reasserting its own national relevance. The AIA at that time included many traditionalist architects hungry for scaled drawings of historic buildings that could inspire their own new designs. Other periodicals included The White Pine journals and also the Beaux-Arts Institute publications that included student work in the classical mode. Simons's book is still available in reprint form called *The Early Architecture of Charleston*. It contains photographs, excellent measured drawings, and a text that vibrantly explains the history and architecture of Charleston.

Fiske Kimball, one of the best-known experts on early architecture in America, as well as being an architect, said of *The Early Architecture of Charleston*, "It is rare that a book prepared for the office use of architects has the historical value of this one."[8] Architect Ralph Adams Cram called the volume a "model," praised the choice of illustrations and types of reproductions, called the measured drawings "invaluable," and approved of every aspect of the book.[9]

At the same time, Simons worked on the issue of the sale of historic interiors to northern museums and collectors at places such as the Metropolitan Museum of Art in New York and what is now the Winterthur Museum in Delaware. Simons's guiding approach was to save building interiors, such as original paneling. If the building was to be destroyed, then the interiors should certainly be saved at all costs.[10] Notable projects where Simons reused architectural elements include the Dock Street Theater and a gas station building, located across from the Fireproof Building, that is now a gift shop for the Historic Charleston Foundation.

There had been a fifty-year foment of the Colonial Revival style (ca. 1880–1930) during which traditionally trained architects would measure and draw scaled architectural drawings of pre-Revolutionary houses. This movement was spurred on by the US centennial celebration in an exposition in Philadelphia in 1876. The buildings highlighted at the event reflected an incipient reverence for Colonial Revival as a patriotic gesture.

By the 1920s the popular illustrated books by Wallace Nutting inspired not only house styles but also furnishings in the Colonial Revival mode. The iconic spinning wheel, a representation of colonial domesticity and productivity, became a common item in many living rooms in the 1920s. This popularity contrasted with the sentiment of Simons's professors at the University of Pennsylvania who looked down on the Colonial Revival style. He found a firm focused on Colonial Revival when he spent a summer in Baltimore for the Laurence Hall Fowler Architecture firm. He gravitated increasingly in that direction once he returned to Charleston. The threat of losing authentic room interiors in Charleston for a short-term financial gain caused the coalescence of Simons and preservation advocates to try to stem the tide of market forces:

> The well-heeled crowd, including tourists, would actually purchase antiques at high prices, while others less wealthy would often buy reproduction Colonial Revival furniture. Following the logic of the movement, wealthy individuals and museums riding the wave of enthusiasm for all things early American were therefore in a frantic search for authentic antique rooms. The paneling, the flooring, the florid plaster ceilings all were sought after as an entirety if possible. Also driving this frenzy in the 1920's was the grand project to recreate the much-changed Colonial capital of Virginia called Williamsburg. Ironically, that project was underwritten by John Rockefeller Jr., whom Charlestonians had

lobbied to save the Joseph Manigault house without much success. In 1927 Simons noted in consternation that the Minneapolis Museum had purchased two Charleston Eighteenth-Century rooms. At least two other houses sold some of their interiors the following year.[11]

Early preservation experts weighed in on preservation issues in Charleston, anticipating an eager pursuit of possessions from the city's past. In the 1920s, William Sumner Appleton Jr. of the Society for the Preservation of New England Antiquities (SPNEA) mentioned that the Metropolitan Museum of Art only accepted interiors of houses that were doomed. Charleston advocates of preservation rallied to discourage the dismantling of structures and interiors that were sound.

A prominent participant in the evolution of preservation in Charleston was Alston Deas. He later completed a monograph on Charleston ironwork. He described the situation in the Roaring Twenties: "The financial Panic had not yet occurred and there was a tremendous amount of money. And everybody and his brother had an idea that they'd get some Charleston souvenir. They were buying ironwork and woodwork and all sorts of things in addition to moveable antiques or nearly moveable ones."[12]

The Charleston Museum was involved in the effort to keep historic architectural elements in Charleston. The museum's director, Laura Bragg, worked hand in glove with the other preservationists in town, especially Simons. He noted that "It distresses me painfully to see our fine old buildings torn down and their contents wrecked or what is more humiliating, sold to aliens and shipped away to enrich some other community more appreciative of things than ourselves."[13]

The prosperity of the 1920s provided the opportunity for Simons & Lapham to design many new and fairly grand houses. Per the planning consultants to the city (the Olmstead brothers from Boston), large areas to the west of the historic White Point Gardens were filled in to extend the peninsula further into the Charleston harbor. This expansion would help meet the growing demand for more downtown houses, many of them graceful brick houses designed in varying permutations of Colonial Revival style. The firm had assisted many homeowners on the peninsula with seamless additions of kitchens and bathrooms, including modern amenities of electrical, plumbing, and heating systems. These were worked into compact, practical houses that conformed with the Colonial Revival style, often with Craftsman touches. In 1920 Albert Simons, in fact, designed his own house at 84 South Battery Street as a Colonial Revival interpretation of a Charleston house with a piazza (an Italian word used in Charleston to refer to a side porch, often roofed) but with Craftsman details.

Additionally, the ethos of the Colonial Revival style locally was strengthened by the conscious role that Simons played in the Charleston

Renaissance—that of a provocateur and leader. Simons's new buildings were designed to be an extension of their historic contexts. His many restorations were subtle and seamless augmentations to the historic architectural context of Charleston. He could not have known at the time that he would have a sixty-year career as the best traditional designer and preservationist in the "Holy City," a nickname for Charleston because of its long history of religious tolerance, evidenced by the many churches and synagogues. However, Simons's long career undoubtedly allowed him the opportunity to shape the city's future. He did so not by obliterating the historic city or imposing modern designs that were unsympathetic to the existing landscape, but rather by constructing buildings that could exist seamlessly with the historic cityscape. This allowed Charleston to remain a living city without abandoning its historic character. The old and the new breathed in harmony.

While other members of the Charleston Renaissance imbibed inspiration from the historic architectural patination so visible in Charleston, Albert Simons brought along his technical and design training, artistic eye, and outgoing personality to coalesce the preservation of not just buildings, but of the broader vantage point of the city. With all the city's twists and exuberant turns, Simons helped in protecting and presenting it for public consumption just as surely as did the images so popularized by Elizabeth O'Neill Verner, Alfred Hutty, and many others.

Verner's book *Mellowed by Time* reflects the great desire Charlestonians had to celebrate the authenticity of their rough-edged city at a time when learned reconstructions such as those of Williamsburg of whom many were wonderful, but not authentic. Unmistakenly Charleston held a European sensibility that appealed to many tourists, and house tours conducted by the Preservation Society of Charleston (and later by the Historic Charleston Foundation) were especially popular. The South Carolina historian Ehren Foley sums it up well:

> As much as any city in America, Charleston is defined by its architecture. The story of the city can be told through its buildings. Its aspirations, its successes, its failures; they are all written on the landscape for those who care to look.... Albert Simons had as much impact on the development of the city's landscape as any figure in the 20th century. This influence came both thorough the design of his own buildings and, even more, from his work as a pioneer of the modern historic preservation movement... Indeed, one might argue that Simons represents something essential to the understanding of Charleston in the 20thcentury.
>
> The tension that existed between innovation and the push to become a cosmopolitan city, set against the pull of tradition and a gaze that could never fully help but look backwards. So Simons, like much of the city, resisted the pull of Modernism and instead worked in the Beaux-

Arts, Classical, and Colonial Revival styles. At the same time, though, he—and the preservation movement generally—was very much a part of the Charleston Renaissance of the 1920s. Preservation as it was deployed in Charleston was not about locking the city in a frozen past, but rather retaining the city's architectural heritage within the context of a living city. That ability was central to rebirth of the city as an international destination by the end of the century. That duality, looking both forward and back at the same time, is quintessentially Charleston and is embodied in Simons's life and career.[14]

Professional Progress

Simons's extensive work on behalf of the AIA at the national, state and local levels allowed for a breakthrough in the annals of preservation in Charleston (for a full listing of Simons's commissions, see Appendix A). Mr. and Mrs. William Emerson of Cambridge, Massachusetts, visited Charleston, and Simons took a great deal of time to show him and his wife around the area. Emerson was head of the department of Architecture at the Massachusetts Institute of Technology (MIT) from 1919 to 1939. Emerson was very impressed with his visit and offered funding for a book on the plantations in the Lowcountry that surrounded the city.

This began a second much-needed book similar to his book on early Charleston architecture in its approach. It contained hard-earned photographs and extraordinary measured drawings as well as explanatory prose from the pens of both Simons and his cousin the quintessential Charlestonian Sam Stoney. The recordation work was enjoyable, often including family picnics at the field sites.

Mrs. Emerson also contributed $500 to the Charleston Museum for buying discarded historic items such as paneling, ironwork and other "architectural beauties" that were being thrown out by a number of Charlestonians. Despite the Emerson's interest and generosity, they ultimately decided to focus their money and efforts on the Heyward-Washington House.[15]

Heyward-Washington House

The Heyward-Washington House located on lower Church Street was the first building focused upon by the community preservationists. The current house replaced an earlier house built in 1770, where George Washington stayed during his southern tour in 1791. The house has three levels and has spectacular, high Georgian rooms, especially on the second floor. The street side of the first floor, however, had been turned into a bakery—the floors had been lowered to ground level, the two rooms

**Heyward-Washington House, 87 Church Street, Charleston (during its time as a bakery).
Historic American Buildings Survey, Library of Congress, Prints & Photographs Division.**

had been stripped of their Georgian moldings and large display windows had replaced the original, mostly brick, first-floor façade.

With the support of Alston Deas, the recently elected president of the Society for the Preservation of Old Dwellings, Simons and Bragg took out a six-month option on the house. That committed them to raise $27,500. At the same time Simons was able to persuade antiquarian Mills Lane of Savannah to purchase some salvaged historic woodwork and ironwork for the Charleston Museum.

Simons and Deas sent out a public appeal for the Heyward-Washington House to raise the funds. Thanks to its fine woodwork and President Washington's visit in 1791, the house had excellent architectural and historical qualifications. William Emerson donated $500 to the project and that built fundraising momentum. He continued to give assistance to the plantation book as well.[16]

Heyward-Washington House, 87 Church Street, Charleston (post-restoration).
Historic American Buildings Survey, Library of Congress, Prints & Photographs Division.

Heyward-Washington House, 87 Church Street, Charleston
(restored second-floor drawing room). Historic American Buildings Survey,
Library of Congress, Prints & Photographs Division.

The Emersons succeeded in securing from their relatives campaign donations to buy and restore the Heyward-Washington House, and Simons completed the architectural drawings and specifications in 1930. The restoration contract documents went room by room explaining in great details the materials, colors, and methods to be used. Charleston Museum President Milby Burton aided with the interior plans. Many layers of paint were scraped back to decide on the colors. Simons noted that there were 2,000 bricks on the lot and that only these historic bricks should be used on the facade's restoration. Before the work was completed, a pre-bakery image of the house, prior to its major changes, unfortunately could not be found. However, Simons's skill and attention to detail resulted in a conjectural restoration that was exactly correct as affirmed by a belated discovery of an early photographic image. Source: Simons & Lapham. Charleston Museum archives.

Heyward-Washington House, 87 Church Street, Charleston
(detail of interior molding). Historic American Buildings Survey,
Library of Congress, Prints & Photographs Division.

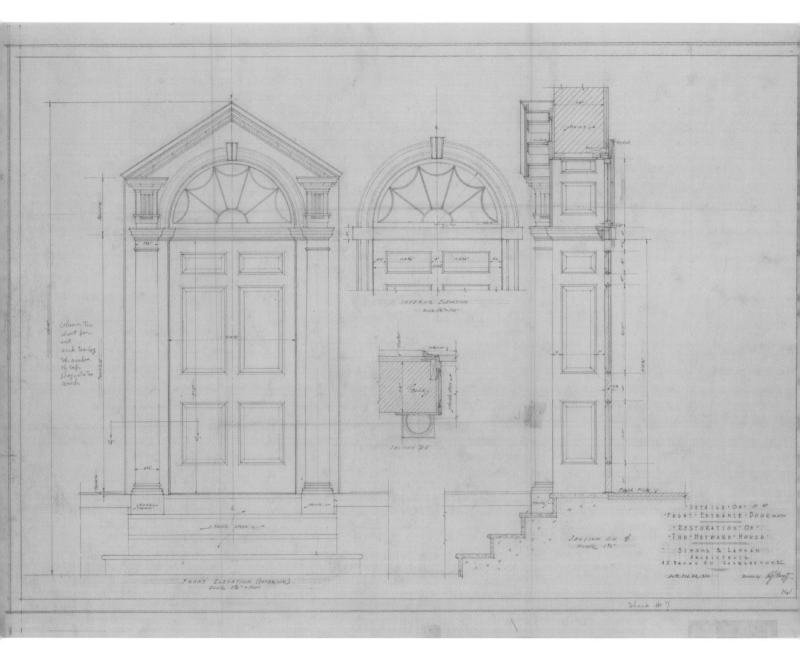

Door and architrave designed by Albert Simons for the Heyward-Washington House.
Courtesy of the South Carolina Historical Society.

Historic District Invented

Mayor Thomas P. Stoney leaned heavily on Simons and his expertise to create a solution to both the problem of losing historic interiors and the bigger threat—filling stations. The Joseph Manigault House was the exemplar for this new threat, having its garden converted to an Esso filling station and being considered for demolition to accommodate a Ford car dealership.

A flash point came when a grand historic structure called the Mansion House (ca. 1772) was in danger of being demolished by a collector of architectural interiors who wanted to gut the building of its original paneled rooms and then demolish what was left. It stood next to St. Michael's church on Broad Street; it was also called the Burrows House and was demolished in 1928. Albert and Harriet Simons wrote an article about it in the 1968 issue of *Winterthur Portfolio*, published by the Winterthur Museum, which has wood paneled rooms from the house.

Mayor Stoney put together a blue-ribbon committee of seven leaders, including Simons, to address the situation.[17] Stoney started with a city council proposal for an ordinance that created a temporary City Planning and Zoning Commission whose principal job was to regulate the placement of new structures, including gas stations, and a "stay of execution" for historic buildings. On April 23, 1929, Mayor Stoney obtained city council approval for this new review process. They soon after took steps toward holding the official rights to review proposed work throughout the historic downtown. They agreed to have a consulting firm for planning the historic district.

A firm from Pittsburgh, Morris Knowles Company, was engaged to study the city and to create a zoning ordinance. They surveyed the architecture and history of the city and they met with neighborhood representatives. They produced recommended boundaries for a new concept (to Americans at least)—the Historic District. It was an area that contained especially pre-revolutionary buildings (Simons said he wished the timespan could have included more later buildings). The new ordinance was ratified by City Council on October 13th of 1931, the first legislation of this type in the United States to receive the full backing of the city government. The Board of Architectural Review had specified roles for some of the members of the board—an architect, an engineer, a real estate broker and a member of the Carolina Art Association.[18]

And, of course, it was not just the buildings that he designed that would shape the city. He also made an impact through his decades of service on the Board of Architectural Review as well as his many other civic endeavors. In addition to the better-known ones are his extensive work with the Carolina Art Association, the local Civic Services Committee, the committee for Safeguarding Charleston Architecture, the incorporation work for the Historic Charleston Foundation, and the battles to save the Robert Mills's Patent Office Building in Washington, which has now become the National Portrait Gallery.

Zoning was still a fairly new concept that was being introduced by a nascent group of planning professionals. Their emerging profession was gaining momentum in the United States and was gaining validation in the courts as an extension of what are known as local governments' "police powers." This meant that the government could legitimately control aspects of use, sizes, and types of buildings in service of the public interest. Planning began at the turn of the twentieth century to combat industrial development, such as manufacturing plants that emitted foul and deleterious exhaust, and ensure that large industry would not be permitted near residential neighborhoods.

By 1931 Charleston had created the Old and Historic District with distinct boundaries. It was the first such district in the country as was the concomitant creation of a Board of Architectural Review (BAR) to oversee all architectural changes in the district, including new construction and demolitions. The new review entity was empowered to approve plans of exterior details on any construction that involved buildings in the area now officially designated by the ordinance as the Old and Historic District. If the proposed alterations or construction met with the approval of the board, a certificate of appropriateness would be issued.

The BAR commenced work almost immediately. Thomas R. Waring, editor of the *News and Courier*, became the chairman. His tact and firmness made the new board acceptable to Charlestonians who valued the property rights of the individual. Albert Simons contributed a great deal of his time as a practicing architect to help ensure that all changes in the historic buildings were appropriate. Within the first year of BAR's operation, Simons was sending Waring lists of applications for alterations along with his comments and drawings for the proposed changes. Simons did express disappointment with the Knowles documents in that they only included buildings constructed before the Revolutionary War. Simons's desire was to lead the property owners to think in terms of paint colors, building materials, and the authenticity of what they were doing, and he set a high bar for the applicants:[19]

> Usually Simons's diplomacy tempered the inclination of the new board
> to swoop down on some organizations or landlords, and instead he
> would revise the applicant's proposed drawing with his own corrections
> to ensure the quality of the design. One example illustrates Simons's
> gentle approach. In a letter to Waring he wrote: "I have suggested to
> Dawson (a board member and an engineer) that similar occurrences
> might be avoided in the future, if the project were discussed with and
> tentatively approved by the Board before the owner and the builder

definitely determined on a scheme. Once a scheme has crystallized in the mind of the owner, he is not receptive to advice and our efforts meet with opposition and frustration. If we could establish our function as advisory rather than disciplinary, I believe that we might count on a larger measure of cooperation from these citizens whom we are attempting to counsel."[20]

By way of an update Simons reported to William Emerson that one year into the use of the new system the situation was as follows:

We have waged successful war against signs and billboards, which is, I suppose, a negative sort of victory. When we have attempted to run a free architectural clinic and advise our citizens how they might carry out their proposed improvements in a better way, we have come face to face with that baffling thing—'invincible ignorance' of architectural propriety. I feel sure it will take a long time to develop a body of public opinion sufficiently strong to make our work really effective.[21]

A Prospering Firm
Architectural Firm of Simons & Lapham

Simons & Lapham was formed by Albert Simons and Samuel Lapham IV (1892–1972) on July 8, 1920. The firm received both local and national acclaim for its work in the areas of architectural design and preservation. The firm continued under the name of Simons & Lapham until 1955, at which time they added a partner to create Simons, Lapham & Mitchell. Later it became Simons & Lapham, Mitchell, Small and Donahue. Their work flourished not only in the 1920s but also in the depression era when they got federal projects.

Lapham was the son of a prominent ice manufacturer and city councilman in Charleston. He graduated from the College of Charleston in 1913 and proceeded from there to earn a BS in architecture from MIT in 1916. While in Boston, Lapham worked for the famous architect Ralph Adams Cram. Lapham served in the US Army during World War I before returning to Charleston where he joined with Albert Simons to form the firm.

In the 1920s the firm was busy with commissions for new houses and restorations, including the thirteen houses in the elite neighborhood of Yeamans Hall. They also added a wing to the main building of the College of Charleston (completed in the early 1930s) and consulted on the restoration of Charles-

Photo of Samuel Lapham, Albert Simons's business partner. Courtesy of E. Blevins.

**Rainbow Row, Albert Simons helped the owner, his client Dorothy Legge,
create the now-iconic color palette in the 1920s.
Courtesy of https://commons.wikimedia.org/wiki/.**

ton's famous Rainbow Row, including working with Dorothy Legge on
the Caribbean colors. During this decade, both partners taught at the
College of Charleston. The firm also completed new plantation-style
houses and restored many others during this time.

In addition to restoring downtown houses, both Simons and Lapham
worked actively with the city government to protect historic buildings.
Simons served on the BAR for approximately 43 years, on the planning
commissions of the City of Charleston, and for Charleston County for 21
years. Simons's commitment was apparent.

Both men were also involved in detailed historic research on Charleston's architecture. They co-edited *The Octagon Library of Early American Architecture, Volume I: Charleston, South Carolina* published in
1927 and republished it under the title, *Early Architecture of Charleston*, which was followed by *Plantations of the Carolina Low Country*
(completed earlier but not published until 1938), along with numerous well-researched articles. Though the first volume for the Octagon
Library sold well, the other nineteen books projected to be completed
thereafter were cancelled. While it was most likely related to the great
depression, architectural historian Gene Waddell's analysis is that

Hope Plantation, restored and altered as a gun club by Albert Simons.
Courtesy of Reggie Gibson, AIA.

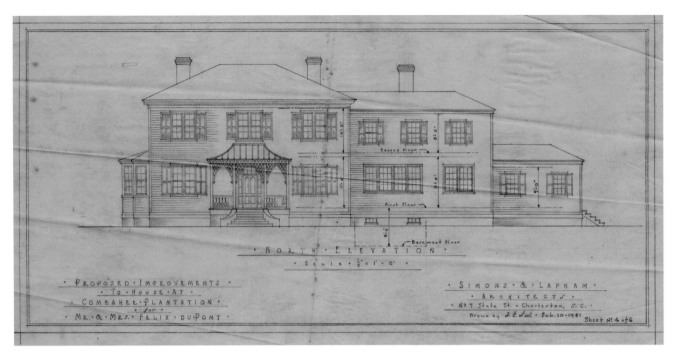

Elevation for Combahee Plantation, restoration by Simons & Lapham for A. Felix du Pont.
Courtesy of South Carolina Historical Society.

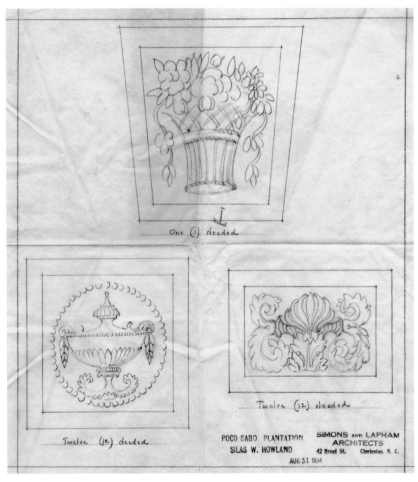

Detail drawings from Poco Sabo Plantation, restoration by Simons & Lapham,
1934. Courtesy of South Carolina Historical Society.

Poco Sabo, ca. 2020 (portico added in 1997). Courtesy of Crosby Land Company.

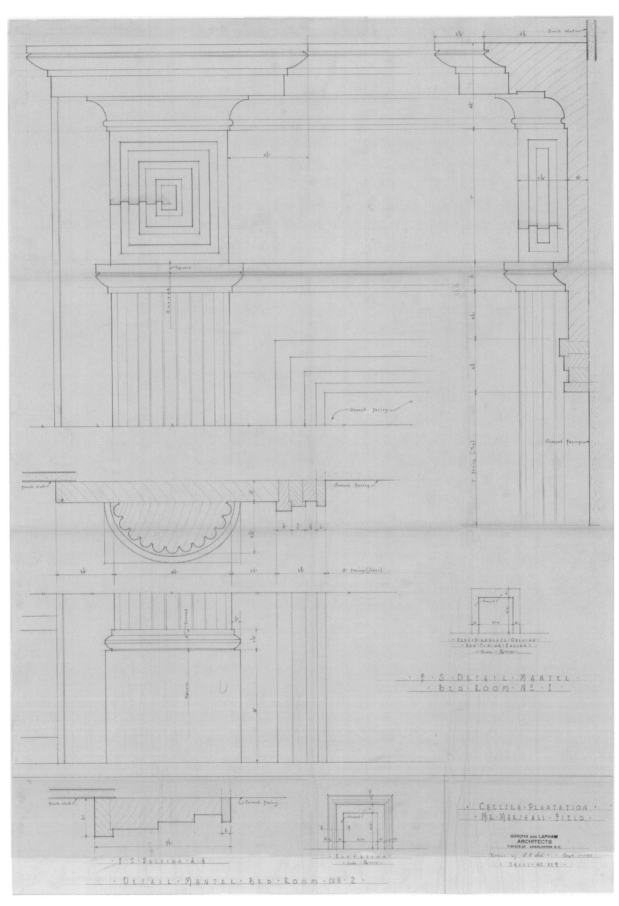

Detail drawings from Chelsea Plantation, design by Simons & Lapham for Marshall Field III 1937. Courtesy of South Carolina Historical Society.

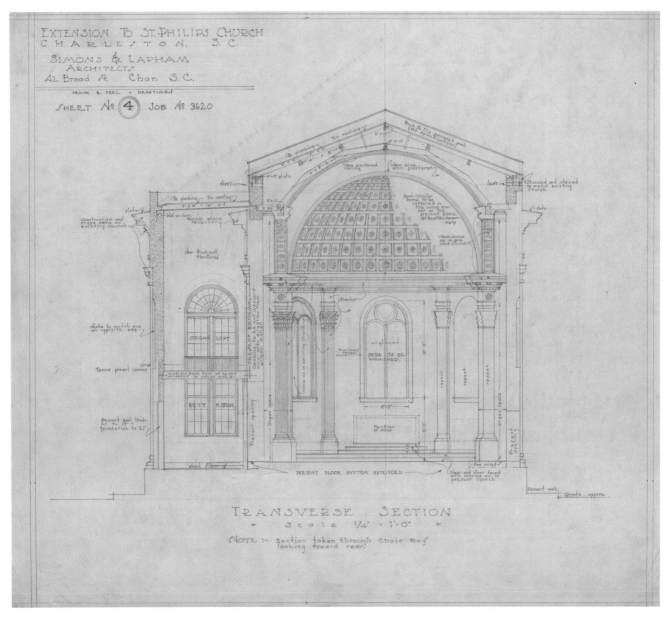

Detail drawings for an extension to St. Philips Church, design by Simons & Lapham. Courtesy of South Carolina Historical Society.

[t]he success of the first volume and the failure of the series reflect the profession of architecture was changing at a crucial moment. For the first time in the history of architecture, the past became irrelevant to the future. Until 1927 a large part of the education of most architects consisted of the study of historic buildings. Architects studied early buildings in colleges, traveled to measure and sketch early buildings, and acquired books with illustrations of early buildings. Their objectives were to equal or surpass buildings that were widely admired. This kind of training was standard when Albert Simons attended the University of Pennsylvania.[22]

Tide Change

While Simons and Lapham found a willing audience in Charleston, they were increasingly swimming against the emerging modernist tide. During the 1920s there was plenty of money for new buildings, but there was an emerging backlash against the pleasant historicist designs that American architecture schools taught. World War I had exposed young architects like Simons to historic European buildings. But after losing that war, Germany suffered severely with runaway inflation and its arts were all affected by the postwar poverty. There was also a new concern with the concept of the Zeitgeist—the spirit of the age. The industrial aesthetic was assimilated in German architectural and other designs.

Pioneers of a new modernist architecture cried foul at the continuation of conventional historicist designs, calling them "false" and deeming them to be exhausted. Leading up to the war there were already artists and designers trying to explore new design norms for an altered era. The iconic painting *The Scream* (1893) by Norwegian expressionist Edvard Munch exemplified the angst-ridden explorations of leading-edge artists that had been mounting in Europe and re-emerged after World War I.

During the war, industrialization had caused a seismic clash between prewar changes in art and design and a new approach that was felt to be purposefully avant-garde and often featured intentionally disturbing images such as those of the German expressionism movement in art. Life had changed. The first global and mechanized war gave birth to military airplanes designed for dropping bombs. Cavalry horses attacked impenetrable tanks and machine guns enriched the kill count. At the same time technology ruled and became a cultural battering ram into a staid architectural bastille.

The German architectural and industrial design school that emerged in the 1920s was called the Bauhaus. In Weimar, Germany, it roiled in the embrace of a new industrial aesthetic for a world overpowered by technological advances and modern materials such as concrete, steel, and glass. The goal was holistic design from dinner forks to public buildings. One director of the school, Mies van der Rohe, quoted Saint Augustine fervently: "Beauty is the Splendor of Truth." The then current high-rise buildings were made of steel frames with cast ornamental skins attached to the frames but not structural. Mies called for the removal of the skin to reveal and revel in the "truth" of the exposed steel.

Once the Nazi party took power in Germany, the Bauhaus was declared decadent, especially because of Jewish faculty in the school. Some of the faculty escaped to America, and there they were welcomed at architecture schools that were increasingly looking toward that "modern" look. A case in point is Joseph Hudnut who was requested to revolution-

People's National Bank Building, 544 King Street, Charleston (1927), with strong classical and Colonial Revival elements. Simons & Lapham continued to design for the city and its surroundings, despite the rising tide of Modernism.

ize the architecture department at Harvard, where he became dean in 1936. He brought the founder of the Bauhaus, Walter Gropius, and the modern designer Marcel Breuer to teach in the Bauhaus manner. Harvard exported both the approach and the imperative for generations of budding professors who carried the modern movement with them to other architecture schools across the United States.

Simons and Lapham collectively published seven articles in *Architectural Forum and Architectural Record* between 1925–1927, while they still accepted historically based designs. These publications were meant to be read by design professionals, yet they were still accessible to the public.

And so Simons and Lapham persisted, despite the rising tide of Modernism. They garnered new design commissions that reflected the penchant for the Colonial Revival style. Unlike Simons's own house that was a permutation of a single house (the distinctive type of house ubiquitous in Charleston), the firm designed houses that were more similar to

**People's National Bank Building pilaster noting
Simons & Lapham ("S&L") along with construction date.**

Colonial Revival designs being built around the country and resembled work being featured in architectural journals and books.

Yeamans Hall

As noted earlier, Yeamans Hall is a particularly interesting community near Charleston built mostly for wealthy northerners, especially those from New York. It was built to be a very private community with a gate (designed by Simons). Simons's association with the Ivy League University of Pennsylvania helped him gain some work on the project alongside the names associated with Yeamans Hall, including Marshall Field and other captains of northern industry. Other than the majority coming from New York, others came from as far away as Colorado and as nearby as the South Carolina upstate, as in the case of textile magnate Roger Milliken. Some already had plantation-style houses in the Carolinas and used their Yeamans Hall houses for socializing. The community was understood to be a part-time place that would allow for balmy wintering with the culture of nearby Charleston to supply entertainment on occasion. The site had been claimed and purchased early in the late seventeenth century by John Yeamans as part of a 48,000-acre grant he received from the King George III of England. He built a house on the property in 1680 that met its demise in a fire in 1888 after being significantly damaged by the great earthquake of 1886.[23]

The unique idea for the snowbird community was that each house should have a large living room to accommodate all members of all designs. The houses encircled a beautiful golf course designed in 1925 by famous golf course designer Donald Ross, and the Olmsted brothers provided a nationally important course design. Henry Getchius, a New

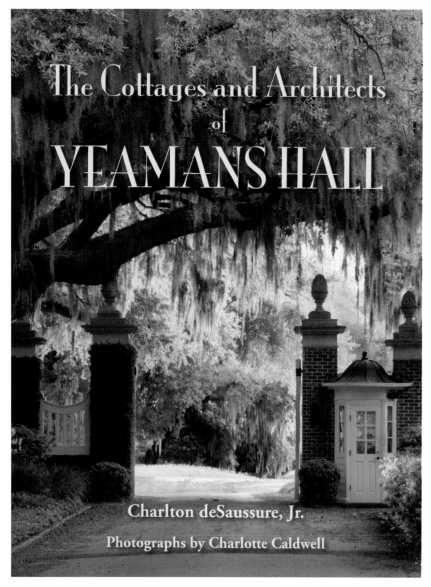

Yeamans Hall book cover featuring the gate and gatehouse by Simons.
Photo by Charlotte Caldwell.

Yorker, had already suggested the idea that the land be used to build a choice winter community there prior to World War I. The 900-acre site still supports thirty-seven residences, the golf course, and some wooded areas for hunting. Northern architects received many of the design contracts, including the famous architect James Gamble Rodgers (1867–1947) from New York who had attended architecture school at Yale and subsequently designed exemplary collegiate gothic buildings at Yale and Columbia Universities.

Albert Simons, though, designed thirteen of the residences, including the Robertson residence and a nonconventional residence for the Colt family, whose company produced pistols. Their house floorplan is shaped roughly like a pistol with the door as the trigger. Like other northern architects, Simons created extraordinarily wonderful traditional designs there. The community still thrives today in its well-designed structures.

The pistol-shaped Colt Cottage at Yeamans Hall, 1931.
Photo by Charlotte Caldwell.

The Robertson Cottage at Yeamans Hall by Albert Simons.
Photo by Charlotte Caldwell.

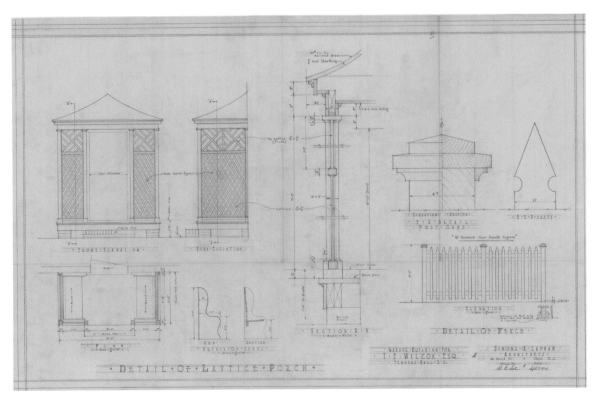

Lattice garden pavilion and details for garage building at Yeamans Hall.
Courtesy of the South Carolina Historical Society.

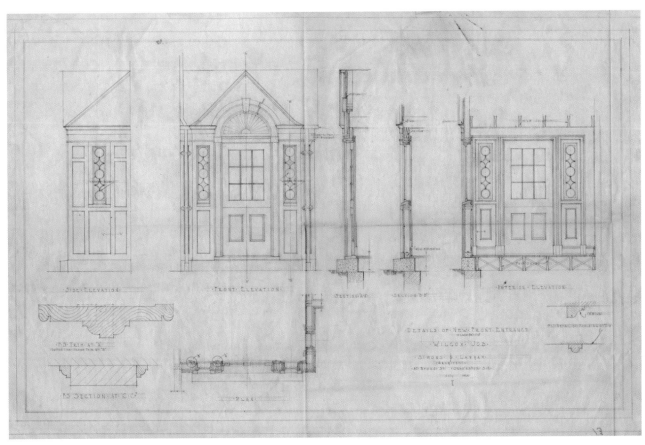

Detail drawings of Wilcox Cottage at Yeamans Hall.
Courtesy of the South Carolina Historical Society.

Etching by Albert Simons, *The Kitchen Gable*

Albert Simons and the Arts in Charleston

Albert Simons was an enthusiastic contributor to the architecture and also, importantly, to the arts of his native city. He joined the Etchers' Club, the Society for the Preservation of Spirituals, and the Poetry Society of South Carolina, which attracted visitors like Gertrude Stein, Robert Frost, Ford Madox Ford, Edwin Arlington Robinson, and John Crowe Ransom.[24] But, of course, it was his work in design and preservation where his contribution provided the most significant impact to the artistic and cultural blossoming that whetted the pallet of artists and writers to create a cultural phenomenon of the arts in Charleston.

Simons exhibited with the Etchers' Club in 1925, 1927, and 1928. Peers included the major Charleston artists Alice Ravenel Huger Smith, Elizabeth O'Neill Verner, Alfred Hutty, and Anna Heyward Taylor. Not surprisingly his work usually featured buildings. "His etchings of foreign scenes were said to display a taste for architecture. In 1928 he exhibited

Place du Calvaire, Rennes

Etching by Albert Simons, *Place du Calvaire, Rennes*

a book plate. Simons became an authority on Lowcountry architectural patterns of the last three centuries and edited and illustrated several books on architecture."[25] The black and white characteristic of etching likely appealed to his architectural background. His etchings were successful, and some are in a collection at the Gibbes Museum of Art in Charleston and at the Charleston Museum.

RUE de BOULLON BREST   albert Simons

Etching by Albert Simons, *Rue de Boullon, Brest*

The Poetry Society of South Carolina was founded in October of 1920, partly in reaction to the criticisms of the South's lack of culture hurled in their direction by the curmudgeonly critic, H. L. Mencken. There was a similar thrust to re-enliven Charleston's traditional role as a center of culture in the South before, and somewhat after, the Civil War. Leading writers and poets in the society were Charleston natives DuBose

Etching by Albert Simons, *Tours*

Heyward, Josephine Pinckney, and Beatrice Witte Ravenel, and from northerly places John Bennett, Alfred Heber Hutty, and William Hervey Allen Jr. "A powerful historical memory shaped the published works of these individuals, most evidently in their characterizations of the region's agrarian commitments, its racial arrangements and its relationship with modernity. By adding their history-laden expressions into the cultural mix at the very moment that other elite groups were doing likewise, Charleston's most productive literati effectively helped fashion a romanticized idea of the city as a place where, in the words of American poet Amy Lowell, 'History touches legend.'"[26]

The editors of the Year Book of the Poetry Society of South Carolina for 1921 included a defining retort to the Mencken shibboleth, "The Sahara of the Bozart"—"As our prime object, we shall strive to work towards the vocal expression of our own part of the United States in any poetic form which carries the message of the poets inspiration…Our only compensation will be the growth of artistic expression in the community."[27]

Whereas previous writers from Charleston, such as the popular Owen Wister, had presented a "genteel Charleston trapped in antebellum amber,"[28] there was a more complex dynamic by the 1920s. That poetry was more experimental in its form and content, though it could never fully separate itself from Charleston's social dynamics. Indeed, one member described the budding group as "one-tenth poetry and nine-tenths 'society'" and DuBose Heyward leveraged his social position to attract members of Charleston's high society, whether or not they were active poets. He simply required that they "be civic-minded and enlightened individuals interested, in the broadest sense of the word, in furthering the art and appreciation of poetry in the community…In no time, the membership list filled with the names of the city's most elite white families…."[29]

Albert Simons had a long and close interest in literature and poetry, as exhibited in some of his personal notes. At the same time he was typically humbled to be a member. "While introducing John Crowe Ransom, the inaugural speaker for the 1928–1929 season, Simons quipped, 'It is indeed an almost overwhelming honor to greet you as President, though for what good reason I should be president, I am somewhat at a loss to understand. Being a poetry society, however, I suppose one should not expect rational interpretation and account for it on the grounds of poetic justice.'"[30]

Looking back on those days, Albert wrote the following in a letter to Abby Howells in January 1974:

> I have a notion that during the years you and John were with us
> Charleston experienced the springtime of a sort of Renaissance notably
> in the work of Dubose and Dorothy Heyward, Josephine Pinckney, the
> Elder Tom Waring, John Bennett and Sam Stoney among the authors
> and Alice Huger Smith and Beth Verner among painters. People from
> other parts of the country were beginning to discover Charleston and
> when they came here tended to broaden our social and intellectual
> horizons. That trend continues today but is not as small and intimate as
> it was then.[31]

**Cartouche (*left*) and Rinceau (*right*) ornaments drawn by Albert Simons.
Courtesy South Carolina Historical Society.**

Architecture has been called "The mother of the arts," and certainly Charleston treated it so. Though it may ironically be a decrepit version of grand old buildings that attracted artists and writers to Charleston, the books and reams of unpublished drawings by Simons contain beautiful, measured drawings carefully laid out and drafted on linen with ruling pens that allowed for a wonderfully chosen set of ink line weights. He may not have been a poet or sculptor, but he certainly considered himself an artist.

Amazingly, Albert Simons also could sing well enough to join an elite group that was organized to archive and perform traditional songs that were otherwise disappearing from the Lowcountry; it was called The Society for the Preservation of Spirituals. Albert designed the logo for the organization and also worked on the archiving and performance of the venerated African American songs.

> Changes in society endangered the survival of the old songs. The group
> gathered the spirituals, learned them, and, in an odd twist, sang them in
> segregated halls, dressed in plantation finery. They sang before President
> Roosevelt and were broadcast on the radio, arousing the admiration
> of the likes of conductor Walter Damrosch. To raise funds to help
> support their mission, their group published a book called *The Carolina
> Low-Country*. It appeared in 1931 filled with the words, poetry and
> images of Charleston Authors, historians, architects and artists...That
> this summation of all things Charleston was really a book on African-
> American culture did not occur to, or seem to bother, Charlestonians...

ironically, their work paved the way for the acceptance of Blacks—in the arts at least—and not just with linkage to the Harlem Renaissance. For while Dorothy and DuBose Heyward sang in the spiritual society; their play *Mamba's Daughters* was making history on Broadway by having the first starring dramatic role for a Black actress, Ethel Waters, by which she launched her acting career.[32]

An Oasis in the Sahara of the Bozart
First Art Courses at the College of Charleston

H. L. Mencken, the famous social critic and witty journalist, famously attacked the American South as being the "Sahara of the Bozart (Mencken deliberately misspelled the French phrase: Beaux-Arts)," claiming they had no notable art museums and lacked in other aspects of cultural blandishments like the ones "up North." Albert Simons and many other southerners highly disagreed with such slander, and Simons took action to combat that image by starting the first art course at the College of Charleston; a directed study in art appreciation. Using glass lantern slides and images pasted on boards, Albert Simons managed to create that new course and taught it from 1924 to 1947.

Albert Simons expressed his feelings about the smear to John Mead Howells on May 28, 1951:

> Dear Albert,
>
> Thank you for your interesting letter and enclosures. I had to take time out to smile at Mencken's crack about the "Sahara of the Beaux Arts." Having heard or invented the phrase he naturally had to pause and look around for an application. "Brookyse" was rather used up "Hollywood" was always good but not applicable -so he used the South. How silly! I wish he had been with me when from Charleston I went over to Atlanta to present the gold medal of the Beaux Arts Society to the department of Arts of U of Georgia [Georgia Tech].
>
> I read the statement to Abby who received the Mencken pronouncement with contempt.

Obviously, the history of architecture was a subject that a young Albert Simons had studied much and had taught at the Clemson architecture school. But his Art Appreciation class at the College of Charleston covered mostly art in a very eloquent manner. Albert focused on the art in its social and political context and used images to bring his points across. Below is an excerpt from his lecture notes that illustrates his pedagogical philosophy:

> "The Romantic Movement in France: The Art of Delacroix, Gericault, Corot, Millet and the Barbizon School."

Some thirty years before the Pre-Raphaelite Brotherhood began its triumphant fight in England for the free expression of new ideals in art, a similar struggle between old and new schools of artists was waged with extraordinary vehemence in France. We have seen how under the revolution and the Empire a cold classicism was the dominating tendency in French painting, and how gradually there arose among younger artists a reaction against this traditional art. The spirit of unrest, which profoundly agitated France after the restoration of the Bourbons and culminated in the revolutionary explosion of 1848, first began to show itself in the art and literature of the younger generation. On one hand were the defenders of tradition, of the "Grand Style" of academic painting, defenders of the classic ideal based on the sculpture of ancient Greece and Rome; on the other were ardent young reformers, intoxicated with the color and movement of life itself, who found their inspiration, not in the classics, but in romantic literature, in Dante, Shakespeare, Goethe, Byron, and Walter Scott. Passion, movement, the imaginative expression of life were the aims of this group of artists that became called the romantics.

LECTURE ON GERICAULT

"Who will deliver us from the Greeks and Romans?" was a catchword among the young enthusiasts who found more beauty in life and nature than in the masterpieces of ancient sculpture. The deliverer was found in the ranks of the reactionaries, in a young artist who was the pupil of Guerin the classicist. Jean Louis Andre Theodore Gericault was born at Rouen in 1791 and came to Paris about 1806, studying first with Carle Vernet and afterwards with Guerin. His method of drawing was so different from that approved by the school of David that it exasperated his "correct" and academic master, who told Gericault that he'd better give up art because it was evident that he would never succeed in it.

One day as Gericault was walking along a road near St. Cloud, a dapple-grey horse in a cart turned restive and plunged about in the sunshine. Gericault whipped out his sketch book and jotted down notes of the movements of the animal and the play of light and shade on his dapple coat, and those notes gave him the idea of a great picture. He would paint an equestrian portrait, not the stiff image of a man on a wooden horse, but a vivid presentment of the plunging, sun-illuminated animal he had seen. He persuaded his friend Lieutenant Dieudonne to pose for the rider, and he had a cab-horse brought round each morning that he might freshen his eye with the points of the horse. Working with the highest enthusiasm and energy Gericault, in the space of a fortnight, produced his, "Officer des Chasseurs a Chevel" now in the Louvre. This picture created a sensation in the Paris Salon of 1812.

**Portrait of Albert Simons by William Halsey. Courtesy of College of Charleston.
Photograph by Heather Moran/College of Charleston.**

Two years afterwards Gericault repeated his success with a companion picture, 'The Wounded Cuirassier,' and after a short period of
military service—when he had further opportunities of studying his
favorite equine models—he went in 1817 to Italy, where he 'trembled'
before the works of Michelangelo, who henceforth became his inspiration and idol.

"When Gericault returned to France in 1818, he found all Paris talking
about nothing but a naval disaster of two years earlier, an account of
which had just been published by two of the survivors. The drama of the

shipwreck of the Medusa seized upon the imagination of the artist, who determined to make it the subject of a picture. He spent months collecting material for his work. He found the carpenter of the Medusa and induced him to make a model of the famous raft by which the survivors were saved. He spent days in hospitals studying the effects of illness and suffering. He persuaded two of the surviving officers of the ship to give him sittings, and painted one leaning against the mast and the other holding out his two arms toward the rescuing ship on the horizon. All his models were taken from life, and it was interesting to note that his friend the famous artist Eugene Delacroix posed for the man who lies inert on the left with his head against the edge of the raft."[33]

What began somewhat as a reaction to a misguided sentiment, grew to become an important School of the Arts for the Southeast. Dr. Diane Johnson arrived in 1970 as both a professor of Art History and as chair of what was then a department of fine arts. A married couple, William Halsey and Corrie McCallum, that taught at the college became good friends with the Albert and Harriet. A portrait of Albert Simons by William Halsey still hangs in the building named for Albert, the Albert Simons Center for the Arts at the College of Charleston. Arts instructors included Emmett Robinson, an actor and playwright who had worked under DuBose Heyward and led the Footlight Players ensemble. Robinson came to the college to create what later became the Theater Department in the School of the Arts.

Etching by John Andrew Burmeister of bridges
with the new bridge under construction.

SIX

RESCUE FROM THE STORM, 1931-1945

Atop mighty pylons towering above the river men in bright helmets swarm like insects performing their task with instinctive skill.

Who first taught the spiders engineering or the wasps architecture? And who instructed the bees to contrive the golden chambers of their storehouses or the ants to make safe their dark tunnels?

Of all the building creatures, man alone is never content with the structures of his forebears, but must ever raise his beams to span wider voids, and at dizzier heights.

Surely here is mastery of space by age old knowledge and courage ever young.

(ALBERT SIMONS, "Reflections on Crossing the Cooper River Bridge," unpublished, 1965)

Fortunately, the past never completely dies for man. Man may forget it, but he always preserves it within him. For, take him at any epoch, and he is the product, the epitome, of all the earlier epochs. Let him look into his own soul, and he can find and distinguish these different epochs by what each of them has left within him.

(FUSTEL DE COULANGES, *The Ancient City,* quoted by Albert Simons in his introduction to *This Is Charleston)*

We should ask of our architects that our buildings be not only of our time but of our place. If we do this we can hope for another age of distinguished Charleston architecture.

(ALBERT SIMONS, *This Is Charleston,* 1964)

The storms that raged in the 1930s and 1940s certainly were linked with the overarching events of the Great Depression and World War II. Architecture also had immense changes occurring during this period. The Bauhaus school in Germany was a design school that widely affected changes in architectural design approaches and building materials. The design aesthetic they pursued was industrial that grew from the mechanization and industrial design utilized during World War I. This melded with austerity measures during both the Depression and World War II to create a very different spare aesthetic. The modernist approach really set in when European modernists like Walter Gropius and Mies Van der Rohe arrived from the German Bauhaus Design School to teach at trendsetting American architecture schools such as Harvard. They were escaping their own political storm in the form of the Third Reich, which declared their work to be decadent.

Political forces also inveighed against the small but effective group of preservationists that included those from old Charleston families. Former mayor John Patrick Grace criticized preservation as the "mania for mummies." In May of 1929, Grace said, "Far be it from me to freeze the genial current of timid souls who now seem satisfied only with memories...If it suits them to mummify Charleston and to make of our city only a museum, let them revel in it. But there should be room enough also for others...Why not awaken with this mercenary reverence for old things also the enterprise that made these old things? Instead of selling the ruins of what they built, why not build something ourselves?...I love the past, but I am living in the present and feel that it is the future to which we must look—even, thank Heaven, as our fathers did."[1]

But even critics like Grace had to admit that the newfound stream of money coming from heritage tourism was burgeoning, and financially strapped homeowners helped sustain an old-world atmosphere that was prized by visitors and artists alike. Deterioration due to their lack of funds played grandly to the crowds, especially as Williamsburg was created. Williamsburg certainly had some authentic architectural fabric, but it also had wide scale recreations with brand new structures, paint, shutters, and any number of other modern interventions.

Surprisingly, the depression decade of the 1930s was extremely busy for Simons & Lapham. They received government contracts when there was little work to be had. Simons went to Washington at the invitation of the US government to serve on committees related to New Deal housing projects. The Robert Mills Manor public housing project, which Simons designed for Charleston in the early 1930s, was one of the first New Deal initiatives for public housing under the Federal Housing Administration (FHA). He also designed a new gymnasium for the College of Charleston under New Deal funding, and, toward the end of the decade, he designed the majestic Memminger Auditorium, which was recently renovated in the late 2000s, and is said to still have the best acoustics in the city. A somewhat less visible but, nonetheless, quite important project was the restoration of the Dock Street Theater and the creation of a new theater in the courtyard of the former hotel. Simons had travelled throughout England to study the appropriate seventeenth-century appearance of the Dock Street theater.

Robert Mills Manor designed by Albert Simons. Robert Mills Housing Project was one of the first New Deal housing projects in the country and noteworthy for its attempt to maintain a design aesthetic that was sympathetic to the character of Charleston's existing architecture. Simons used high-quality, long-lived materials such as tile on the roofs, lock-seam copper pent roofs, cast iron, and recycled bricks. Historic American Buildings Survey, Library of Congress, Prints & Photographs Division.

Old gym at College of Charleston, designed by Simons
under a Works Progress Administration (WPA) commission.

The Dock Street Theater. Historic American Buildings Survey,
Library of Congress, Prints & Photographs Division.

Dock Street Theater Adaptive Reuse

The Dock Street Theater project was an exciting one for Simons. The Planter's Hotel at 135 Church Street was built (ca. 1800) on a site that included the former early American theater called Dock Street Theater (later the street name was changed to "Queen Street"). The earliest play officially performed in the theater was, *The Recruiting Officer* in 1738. Scant records exist after 1740, thus the archives may have fallen victim to the great fire of 1740. The Planter's Hotel famously prospered in the first half of the nineteenth century but shared the economic malaise of postbellum Charleston. The preservation movement in Charleston emphasized the high-profile location of the Planter's Hotel and the historic importance of the Dock Street Theater at that location. The city was eventually convinced to buy the inn and convert it to a theater. In the mid-1930s financial support was provided for that option by the Federal Emergency Relief Administration and toward the end of the project it received funding from the Works Progress Administration (WPA).

At the opening ceremony for the Dock Street Theater Mayor Maybank said:

> The story of something lost saved from a past, which might have been forever lost. And it is the story, too, of the saving of human values, for the labor that made this restoration was relief labor—the work of hands which might otherwise have been idle. The work which these hands have done, guided by the nation's best architectural knowledge, will remain a source of intimate satisfaction to those who come to Charleston as visitors as well as those who have, year by year, in their daily footsteps, passed by the ruins of a rare inheritance . . . Suffice it to say that the work, from top to bottom, was a work of harmony and of love, and of determined, resolute knowledge and spirit.[2]

Albert Simons studied eighteenth-century English theaters and designed a new theater to fit in the courtyard of the old Planter's Hotel based on those approaches. The layout with balcony boxes and restrained but evident carvings and referential detailing give the theater a rich and appropriate appearance. The majority of the woodwork is made from local cypress trees. Previously doomed woodwork from the Radcliff-King house was salvaged by Simons and used in the upstairs reception room.

In 1939, Simons noted, "During the Depression, Charleston has been kept going by the throng of tourists who have come here during the winter months. At the present time presidents of banks and of the Chambers of Commerce and of Rotary and of whatnots are all fanatical for preservation. Like all converts, they are more Royal than the King, more Catholic than the Pope, and want to preserve everything that is owned

Dock Street Theater, exterior, 1937. Carnegie Survey of the Architecture of the South, Library of Congress, Prints & Photographs Division.

Dock Street Theater, stage, 1937. Carnegie Survey of the Architecture of the South, Library of Congress, Prints & Photographs Division.

Dock Street Theater, seating and balconies, 1937. Carnegie Survey of the
Architecture of the South, Library of Congress, Prints & Photographs Division.

Dock Street Theater, interior, 1937. Carnegie Survey of the Architecture of the
South, Library of Congress, Prints & Photographs Division.

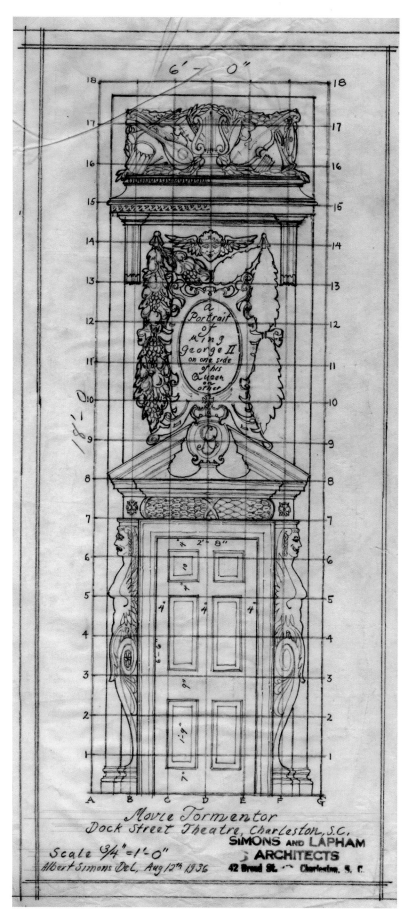

Drawing for Dock Street Theater door.
Courtesy South Carolina Historical Society.

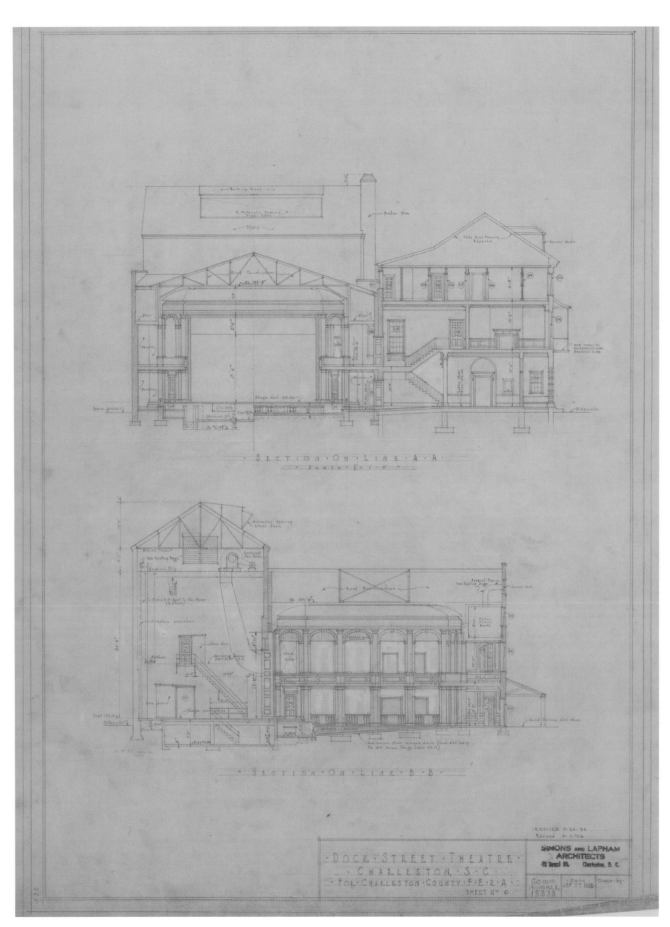

Plans for the Dock Street Theater showing the auditorium placed in the courtyard of the old Planter's Hotel on Church Street. Courtesy South Carolina Historical Society.

by somebody else, whether good, bad or indifferent. Should the tourist trade lapse, their interest would evaporate." The swarms of Yankee snow-birds included E. F. Hutton, Solomon Guggenheim, and other wealthy founders and scions of business. Simons had connections to northeast-erners from having attended the University of Pennsylvania. Simons did a lot of impressive work for the northerners, nicknamed "Yankee Plant-ers," especially those who came south for winter recreation in the form of hunting and golfing.

Simons was quoted as saying, "working so hard for a hoard of out-landers…I am getting quite fed up with millionaires," yet he had few local clients and therefore needed the work associated with the thriving northeastern economy. On a selective list of twenty-six city and country residences on which Simons & Lapham worked in the 1920s, twenty-two were owned by northerners from such places as New York, Pennsylva-nia, Connecticut, and Massachusetts. Whatever Simons's personal feel-ings about millionaires or Yankees, the reality remained that without the influx of northern money, many of the Charleston properties that Simons held so dearly may have deteriorated beyond repair.[3]

Major northern players in supporting preservation in Charleston were William and Frances Emerson of Boston. As mentioned, William Emerson, a relation to Ralph Waldo Emerson, was the head of the De-partment of Architecture at MIT. His father was William Ralph Emerson, one of the architects who created what was later dubbed, "The Shingle Style." William and Frances gave and raised money for preservation in Charleston and provided financial support for the book *Plantations of the Carolina Low Country* that Simons and his eccentric brother-in-law Sam Stoney were working on. The Emersons gave money toward the preservation of the Joseph Manigault House and the Heyward-Washington House in 1927. By 1930 Mrs. Emerson was still very much involved and financially supported preservation in Charleston. She paid to start an American Institute of Architects committee for safeguard-ing Charleston, which included predictable locals such as Simons and Deas as well as national figures including Fiske Kimball and Leicester Holland.

In 1939 Robert Whitelaw, a civic leader, expanded the committee to include Sam Stoney, E. Milby Burton, and Alice Ravenel Huger Smith. They called upon Frederick Law Olmsted Jr., who was one of the top planning and landscape experts and he recommended a more complete survey of the architecture. Hence the committee members above were called upon to help with what would become the publication, *This Is Charleston*. Olmsted also created the innovative idea called a revolving fund, a preservation tool in which the preservation organization would buy a dilapidated but historic house, pay to fix it up, sell it for a higher price with a deed covenant that disallowed quick resale, and require adequate maintenance by the homeowner. This fund structure was how Ansonborough in Charleston was restored en masse.

At the same time, the arts and historic atmosphere drew tourists to Charleston for reasons ineffable. As Stephanie Yuhl put it, "Charleston historian Sam Stoney conveyed an intensely personal and emotional connection to the city's buildings that went beyond mere aesthetic appreciation—they were part of the 'legacy of memory' that elite locals were duty-bound to protect and pass on. In Charleston, he reasoned, 'How is a man to describe with any form of accuracy those things and those ways of living and thinking that after a fashion are more intimately parts of him than his feet and hands, his tastes or his abilities? The difficulty that comes from being a Charlestonian is that the things and thoughts, the memory and the manners that make up the Charleston that count are too completely part of one's heart and one's soul to be realizable…Charleston is largely a matter of feeling.'"[4]

Samuel Gaillard Stoney was the brother of Albert's wife, Harriet, and was quite an active lecturer and writer. He collaborated with Albert and would join the couple on weekend family visits to historic plantation sites. Like another earlier plantation site expert, Judge "Ham" Smith (the nickname stood for "Henry Augustus Middleton") who had an obsessional interest in plantations and their boundary lines and configurations, Sam Stoney contributed much knowledge and energy to the study of Lowcountry plantations both in his written works and in his expertly drafted maps and drawings. A look back at the days of plantation explorations is recounted by Harriet in a page in the book *Plantations of the Carolina Low Country* entitled "How the Book Was Made":

> It was inevitable; too many people in the Low Country saw that such a thing to be done. In 1928 many of these old houses were at such a low ebb of survival that a visual recording of them was needed at once.
>
> That spring a generous spirit, William Emerson of Boston, put heart into the project by offering financial aid the services of an excellent photographer. The editors, who had already gained considerable knowledge of the houses in their practice, began plans for the book. In the winter Ben Judah Lubschez took a very full set of photographs and work was begun on the layout of the book.
>
> Work was started also to get the records the camera could not make. Time was snatched from busy lives to explore and measure for elevations and plans. Sunday after Sunday the parties went out. Sometimes it was lone men or a team of them. Sometimes there were grandly mixed parties of men, women and children. Everyone worked; the men with their grandiloquent gestures of machetes clearing underbrush grown second story high, the women with soon toughened thumbs pressing

Memminger Auditorium, 56 Beaufain Street, Charleston.

the ends of the tape crumbling walls, the children clearing trash and rubbish so that the buried corners could be found and lost partitions located.

Thus we covered houses and churches in fair order, and buildings only piles of earthquake rubble, gardens in full glory, and gardens hidden under scrub pine and snaky briar patches; all were measured and their plans delineated. Probably the workers enjoyed the ruins most, because each could speculate gloriously on the details that were hopelessly lost.

Then when the book was ready for publication the depression stopped everything. For years the project remained a determination in the mind of Albert Simons. At last in 1938, ten years after its beginning, ways were found.[5]

Plantations of the Carolina Low Country was an unqualified success even during the Great Depression. Financial support for its publication came from the Carolina Art Association and the American Council of Learned Societies.

Memminger Auditorium

Perhaps the most important architectural design that Albert Simons created for Charleston is the Memminger Auditorium on Beaufain Street. It is designed with a spare but perfectly proportioned form and with an antis in muris portico similar to one used by his college mentor, Paul Philippe Cret, as seen in the Rodin Museum on the grand parkway in Philadelphia. The auditorium also bears a strong resemblance to the Monumental Church in Richmond, Virginia, by one of Albert Simons's favorite architects, Robert Mills. Simons's drawings include numerous full-sized details to ensure an exactitude of execution for details throughout the building.

The building was constructed for the former Memminger School, which was a private girl's school near the middle of the city. The architecture of the school was Mediterranean Revival, built in the 1910s. The auditorium by Simons was completed in the 1930s to benefit both the Memminger school students and to provide a venue for the public as well. Many older Charlestonians recall piano recitals, tap-dancing events, plays, and musical performances.

Bell Building by Philip Tramwell Schutze

Regarding the new Bell Building on Saint Philip Street by Phillip Tramell Schutze of Atlanta, Simons wrote:

> Rome has remained the eternal city because it has maintained its spiritual and cultural ties with its past. A palace of the sixteenth century does not look out of place beside a church of the thirteenth century or a mouldering arch of the second century. Harmony with the local scene prevails and the past and present are in accord. This is seldom the case with us: our cheaper dwellings and most of our commercial buildings might just as well be found in Detroit or Las Angeles, so devoid are they of anything resembling local significance.
>
> However, I would like to invite your appreciative attention to the new Bell Telephone building on St. Philip Street, as a highly efficient modern building graciously in accord with its surroundings. I hope that we may detect in this building the beginning of a more liberal and enlightened policy in those responsible for our commercial architecture.

Schutze, the designer of the Bell Building to which Simons refers, was consciously paying homage to the work of William Mason Smith House at 24–26 Meeting Street. The spare surfaces and Greek detailing are consonant with the Meeting Street house, which was designed by William Jay. An Englishman, Jay was trained in London during the short-lived Regency period of design and worked in Charleston and Savannah during his relatively brief stay in America. Schutze was a contemporary of Simons, having also been born in 1890 (passing two years after Simons in 1982) and was considered one of the foremost Classical architects in the country. He attended architecture school at the Georgia Institute of Technology and later was awarded the Rome Prize (the most coveted prize in architecture in that day and still a great honor). While in Rome he made daring trips up many high ladders to measure great buildings so that he could draw them for recordation but even more so for later references in his own classical design work. His greatest contribution to design in his lifetime was his proclivity for the Italian Baroque as an inspiration for many of his works, especially mansions in the Atlanta suburbs, most notably the Swan House (now a house museum open to the public).

He also designed medieval-themed houses and applied other approaches to urban buildings. He worked for the firm of Heinz, Reid & Adler for many years. A consistent client of the firm was the Bell Telephone company, thus the Bell Building on the College of Charleston campus was his only building in Charleston.

Recording the Old, Creating the New

In addition to completing measurements and exquisite drawings of historic buildings that he greatly admired, Simons also coordinated the Historic American Building Survey (HABS) for the Southeastern states in the 1930s. It was a New Deal program to put professionals to work recording historic buildings with photography and measured drawings. This program was created in 1933 by Charles Peterson, and it was coordinated by the National Park Service and is still very active today. The books by Simons and his collaborators were exactly the sort of well-drawn architectural drawings that the HABS program specified for its recordation teams. The accepted projects continue to be placed in the Library of Congress with all the earlier projects.

During this time (1930–1945), Albert worked with his brother-in-law Samuel Stoney in the creation of the book *Plantations of the Carolina Low Country*. The book includes beautiful, measured drawings and photographs of plantations in the area and a text that has many interesting insights into the architecture and the history of the Lowcountry in general. The Simons and Stoney families would sometimes picnic at the sites that were being studied.

Many were interested in the struggling and sometimes abandoned plantation houses. Simons worked on many of the old plantations, often equipping them with kitchens and bunk beds so that they may be used by hunters as a base camp. Most of those who stayed were northerners traveling south for the long hunting seasons. An example of this phenomenon was the arrival of a group of New Yorkers by boat at Fairfield Plantation in 1900: "When the party entered the house, they found it was uninhabitable. Plaster had fallen from the leaky ceilings onto the beds. Windowpanes were broken. Dust was an inch thick. It looked as if no one had been there in recent times. The group was glad that no tuxedos had been brought."[6]

Despite such disappointments, northerners continued to come down and buy and fix up old plantations, often embracing Lowcountry ways. The wildlife and mild winters made for excellent hunting conditions, including hunts for duck, wild turkey, deer, fish, boar, quail, and other game. At Hobcaw Barony, the Wall Street tycoon and presidential advisor Bernard Baruch owned 12,000 acres and numerous structures. He hosted many notable individuals including ambassadors, senators, captains of industry and wealth, and even Winston Churchill and (separately) Franklin Delano Roosevelt, who oversaw the US government and war efforts from a car phone during a month-long stay at Hobcaw Barony. Similar wealth begat new life in many other plantations and islands, including the Guggenheims at Daniel Island near Charleston, and other islands extending down the Georgia coast bought by wealthy northern families with names such as Rockefeller and Kennedy.

One such family was the couple Victor and Marjorie Morawetz, well-connected and wealthy philanthropists from New York. The Morawetzes relocated to Charleston in the late 1920s and moved in many of the same social circles as Albert Simons, including having a close relationship with Josephine Pinckney. They engaged Simons in their project to restore the Pink House at 17 Chalmers Street, a former tavern thought to be among the oldest buildings on the peninsula. An even larger project followed when the couple purchased Fenwick Hall, an early eighteenth-century plantation home on Johns Island. Simons worked to maintain the historic character of the home while simultaneously bringing modern amenities like electricity, plumbing, and a pool house that stood adjacent to a large saltwater swimming pool with water pumped in from the nearby Stono River.[7] Simons also brought some of his characteristic Colonial Revival styling to the project, most noticeable on the redesigned main entry door.

Both Albert Simons and Samuel Lapham served voluntarily in the military for two years during World War II, and during this time they

The Pink House, 17 Chalmers Street, Charleston, 1933.
Historic American Buildings Survey, Library of Congress,
Prints & Photographs Division.

Fenwick Hall, Johns Island, 1938. Historic American Buildings Survey,
Library of Congress, Prints & Photographs Division.

Fenwick Hall, detail of entryway, redesigned by Simons
with strong Colonial Revival elements, 1938. Historic American Buildings Survey,
Library of Congress, Prints & Photographs Division.

Fenwick Hall, mantle detail, 1938. Historic American Buildings Survey,
Library of Congress, Prints & Photographs Division.

Watercolor of Fenwick Hall by Anna Heyward Taylor, 1930.

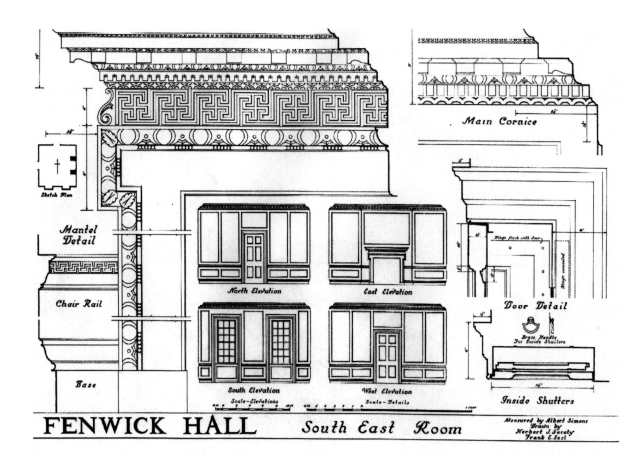

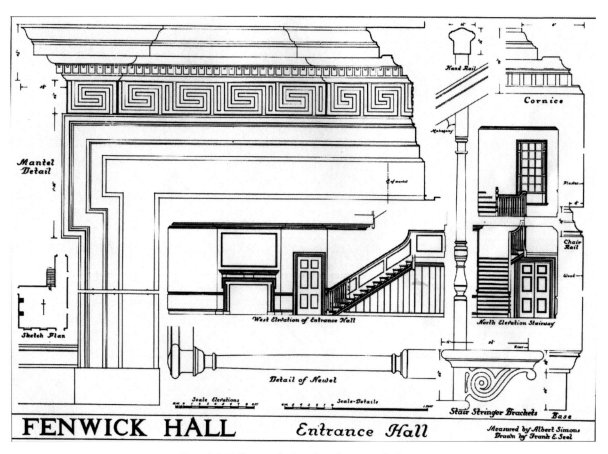

Fenwick Hall recordation drawings, analytique.

Ainsley Hall House (Robert Mills House), Columbia, SC, pre-renovation image, 1934.
Historic American Buildings Survey, Library of Congress,
Prints & Photographs Division.

Ainsley Hall House (Robert Mills House), Columbia, SC, post-renovation image,
1970. Historic American Buildings Survey, Library of Congress,
Prints & Photographs Division.

Albert Simons with plans at Ainsley Hall House (Robert Mills House), Columbia, SC.
Courtesy of Historic Columbia.

shuttered the firm. Simons served as a major in the US Army Corps of Engineers at Liverpool and Le Havre. After the war the firm reopened and grew as postwar commissions flowed in, including the Charleston Municipal Airport, the Law School Building at the University of South Carolina, and the restoration of two buildings designed by Robert Mills: the Fireproof Building and Ainsley Hall House in Columbia, South Carolina.

This Is Charleston

Albert Simons wrote the introduction to the survey book of downtown Charleston architecture. He and Helen McCormack, at the behest of Frederick Law Olmsted Jr., had started a survey of historic houses on the peninsula. Albert Simons, John Mead Howells, Alice Ravenel Huger Smith, and Sam Stoney were the "judges" who weighed in on the importance of each historic house with 1,168 properties surveyed. They were then ranked in one of five categories:

1. Nationally Important
2. Valuable to the City
3. Valuable
4. Notable
5. Worthy of Mention

Both Albert Simons and Samuel Lapham worked on the survey of Charleston architecture that led to the creation of *This Is Charleston*, which was published in 1944. A team of four drove throughout Charleston evaluating the level of importance of the buildings in the historic parts of the city. Helen McCormack did yeoman's work on the survey, and John Mead Howells, Albert Simons, Alice Ravenel Huger Smith, and Sam Stoney reviewed the buildings, comparing notes on the categories that they decided to award to individual structures.

An example of the team comments on the survey cards was an entry that was a large early Victorian building: Alice Ravenel Huger Smith: "a well-built house of a poor type." Stoney: "Mention." Simons: "This house is an outstanding example of megalomania which had already infected our domestic architecture before the war. The war did not cause the decline of taste but only arrested its expression. This decline in taste came with the Industrial Revolution and was universal throughout the western world. Its most distressing feature besides the coarseness of its ornament is the loss of any sense of human scale." Notable (as a type). Howells: "a dignified example of its type."

There was some levity in the comment cards as well, for example:

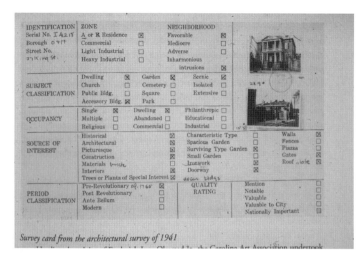

Survey card from *This Is Charleston* architectural survey.

Smith: "Georgian Period III, p. X pl 14, Octagon Lib, Dwelling Houses p. 222"; Stoney: "Valuable (I was born there)"; Simons: "Valuable to the City (in spite of nativity of SGS (Stoney))"; Howells: "Has lovely drawing room 2nd floor and an authentic ghost."[8]

Below is Albert's introduction to *This Is Charleston*, surveyed 1940–1941 and prepared for publication (alongside a public gallery show) in 1944. It shows the duality of his mind and his willingness to think and plan for the future even while he documented and preserved the past. These two traditions, he insisted, were not in opposition, but rather could exist in harmony if Charlestonians embraced a spirit of structured planning:

> No Charlestonian can be expected to speak or write about his city objectively for it is so much a part of the background of his mind and emotions that detachment is never possible. The lovely and the shabby are all woven into the same warp and woof of the familiar scene. The stucco facade of some old house, its chalky colors weather-faded, its surface mapped with earthquake patches and crumbling at the windows, through a sort of empathy assumes a character akin to an aged face looming out of one of Rembrandt's later portraits, infinitely world-weary yet infinitely enduring and wise in human experience.
>
> New buildings do not have this quality and seldom acquire it in the lifetime of their builders, and those of shoddy construction without basic integrity achieve this distinction not at all and do not deserve our veneration simply because of age.
>
> It is generally conceded among architects that with the lapse of every ten years there is an appreciable change in the style and manner of building.... Of course, the earlier buildings with the unmistakable cachet of the 18th century will always surpass all others in their quality of

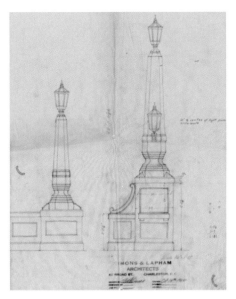

Ashley River Bridge,
drawing of lamp post by Simons

Ashley River Bridge lamp post.

workmanship, but with the early 19th Century came a greater variety and
invention in planning and in the forms of enclosed space....

By and large Charlestonians had reverted since World War One to
what is generally believed to be "Colonial," sometimes descending to
the meretricious, variety and as often as not flavored with extraneous
elements borrowed from Williamsburg, Cape Cod, or stock millwork.
While not entirely satisfactory to the fastidious, the general effect is not
inharmonious in its setting.

What of the future? Without claiming to possess the gift of prophecy,
there are certain facts that are discernable before us.... from the earliest
times private ownership of all the land north of Beaufain Street and its
subsequent development as separate boroughs precluded the achieve-
ment of any comprehensive plan for the growth of the city. Today this
lack of a workable plan has become more obvious with the lapse of time.

With three bridges across the Ashley River and a second bridge
now being built across the Cooper, an east-west National Defense
super-highway to terminate at Charleston, and another north-south
artery to pass nearby are all factors which intensify the already acute
traffic problems arising from the crazy-quilt patterns of streets inherited
from unguided private enterprise of ante-bellum days. Fortunately, the
rerouting of streets south of the city limits can be accomplished without
sacrifice of any buildings of major interest. But comprehensive planning
should not be postponed indefinitely....

In our justifiable preoccupation in preserving worthy survivals from
the past, we have to some extent excluded the immediacy of the present
and of the imminent future. Many worthy Charlestonians, whose
motives are above question, view with alarm the erections on our sacred

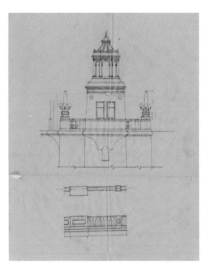

Ashley River Bridge, drawing of minder's house by Simons.

Ashley River Bridge, oblique view of the bridge-minder's house.

soil of any building designed in the contemporary manner. This does not follow, however, the traditions of our forefathers whose architecture was fully abreast of that of the rest of the country and often in the forefront, but always tempered by climate, custom and local preference.

After a couple of generations of experimentation and controversy, modern architecture has achieved orthodoxy throughout the civilized world although it has given rise to a great variety of sectarians. With its establishment it has naturally grown more conservative and responsible. It will in time grow more gracious, more urbane and more attuned to human emotions, and Charlestonians should prepare themselves for its acceptance but on their own terms. We should ask of our architects that our buildings be not only of our time but of our place. If we do this we can hope for another age of distinguished Charleston architecture.

Albert Simons, 1964

The bridges that Simons referenced were an apt metaphor and, indeed, he had helped to design the Ashley River Bridge, which had opened in 1926. They brought commerce and prosperity, helping to open the city to the world and allowing traffic, goods, and people to flow in and out of Charleston. They were part of the infrastructure that made Charleston a modern city. But in Simons's design, he harkened back to classical detail, looking backward while simultaneously helping the city to enter into the somewhat new century.

TRANSCENDED LIMITS, 1946-1980

What is there in the list of strange and unexpected events that has not occurred in our time? Our lives have transcended the limits of humanity; we are born to serve as a theme of incredible tales to posterity.

    (AESCHINES, *Oration Against Ctesiphon,* 330 B.C.E., as recorded by Albert Simons in a notebook of quotations)

Today we are the heirs of the ages and have access to all styles, but we should strive to use them with discretion and only when they accord with the character and purpose of the building.

    (ALBERT SIMONS on architectural education)

I have been reading Toynbee's "Study of History" which at least gives this consolation that, however terrifying the present may be, much worse things have already happened in the past.

    (Letter from ALBERT SIMONS to John Mead Howells, July 31, 1947)

Albert Simons was well aware of the societal and global venues showcasing recent and modernist designs. By the late 1940s Albert Simons found an amazing continuation of his work despite his absence to serve in World War II. He even went so far as to say that his airport design for the first Charleston airport was perhaps his favorite design, though for him it was a rare modern design executed within a tight budget. It still aligned with the rather restrained lines of such buildings at that time. Having seen duty in two world wars and the many precedents for simplified modernist designs, this building probably had special meaning for Albert, representing both joy at the usefulness of an airport but melancholy about the ascendant modernism elsewhere.

Charleston Airport, designed by Simons.

The quoted letter below shows Albert's awareness that the huge changes of the twentieth century were enormous in their impact and, amidst the scientific ethos, hard to comprehend. While the years of the 1950s are often grouped together as a sweet and mellow period in American life, Albert, now in his sixties, felt the restless tug of the scientific revolutions that had emerged in American society. But he did not feel he had much to learn from the architectural experiments of the preeminent architects of that time—people such as Edward Durell Stone, Wallace K. Harrison, and Gordon Bunshaft of Skidmore, Owings & Merrill.

In a letter to his long-time confidant John Mead Howells from August 1950, Simons mused about the rate of change and its almost overwhelming quality. "I have just been reading Gerald Johnson's "Incredible Tale," a summary of our American history during the last fifty years," he reported, "What stupendous events we have lived through! Is there any wonder that most of us feel a bit weary with no desire for more world drama?"

But changes in architecture, as well as in other areas of American life, arrived quickly in the postwar period. A new ubiquity of modernism arrived in the form of suburban sprawl, with its automobile-oriented

Herbert DeCosta, contractor and long-time collaborator of Simons.

culture and banal strip shopping centers that essentialized Bauhaus modernism into a cheap, simple way of constructing the public realm but lacking proportions and details.

Albert Simons was ambivalent about the emergent Modernism in the architectural designs of his day. He personally felt that the fine historical precedents leave plenty of room for creativity while contributing greatly to the aesthetic continuity of fine and recognized forms and proportions.

In this 1949 letter to his former employer in Baltimore, Laurence H. Fowler, Albert wrote:

> Having just come from a session of the jury of fellows where most of the best work submitted was definitely aligned with modernism, it was a pleasure to visit your library and renew my acquaintance with the great men of the past who have made architecture such an eloquent expression of the human spirit.
>
> I have no quarrels with modernists, in fact, I admit that what they are doing is almost inevitable in this age that is almost wholly scientific. Much modern work is extremely romantic, almost melodramatic in fact, but there is very little poetry of enchantment in any of it. I have no doubt that this deficiency will one day be restored. Then students will again seek the councils of the great men of the past and the study of their thinking will enrich our work with that sense of beauty now absent.

But developments in the architectural landscape were not the only changes that Simons noted in his letters. He also took a stance of support for the advancement of African American people in a place and at a time when such attitudes were far from given. He worked closely with the outstanding African American contractor Herbert DeCosta who was known for his meticulous restorations and attention to detail in both new work and in restoration work.

Simons worked on many projects with Herbert DeCosta, who was a third-generation contractor in Charleston and a frequent collaborator on Simons's construction projects. DeCosta's grandfather, Benjamin DeCosta, started the firm then called DeCosta and Edwards, which was headquartered on State Street. His father, Herbert DeCosta Sr., began working for his father's company after graduating from the Avery Institute in Charleston only taking a break to serve in World War I. DeCosta Sr. was known as an excellent contractor as well. Herbert DeCosta Jr. joined his father's firm in 1947 and became the head of the company upon his father's death in 1960. Both he and his father worked on projects across the state, with some projects having multi–million-dollar budgets.[1]

Historian Martha Severens notes Albert and Harriet's liberal racial views along with Albert's support of programs for the advancement of African American people. Simons wrote:

> There is in Charleston a small foundation...who award fellowships
> to promising young Charlestonians for advanced study in the fields of
> literature, science, and the arts. Recently a fellowship was granted to
> Merton D. Simpson, a young Negro artist, who has received his first
> training from a local artist. A few days ago it was announced that four
> Negro officers would be assigned to the municipal police force. Certainly
> these are things that should be done.

Harriet and Albert: Champions for Social Justice

While Albert Simons worked extensively for the good of the architectural profession (working, as he did, on the American Institute of Architects as an officer and as an itinerate lecturer), his wife Harriet worked tirelessly as a leader and member of organizations for the betterment of Charleston during the Great Depression, and then as an extremely active part of the war effort in Charleston and across the state. She corresponded widely with governors and a great many others to attempt to improve Charleston even amidst the economic turmoil of the 1930s that allowed for degrading conditions throughout the Lowcountry. Just as she had led the state branch of the League of Women Voters, she maintained a vocal leadership role in "cleaning up" areas to lower crime and at the same time desiring to help unwed mothers and to teach birth control, to educate the masses on the dangers of venereal diseases, and to exhort the enforcement of laws to limit debauchery, especially at the Charleston Naval Base, the main employer in town.

An example of her involvement and leadership is her creation of the organization in Charleston called the Civic Union. Ignited by the news of a murder in a restaurant, Harriet and others called for a public forum to urge betterment in many areas of city life.[2] Six-hundred citizens attended the meeting, which was held at the gymnasium of the High School of Charleston. *The Evening Post* (Charleston) report of the event included the following:

> Mrs. Albert Simons, Vice-President of the Civic Union, observed that if the establishments mentioned were not fit for soldiers to visit they were certainly not fit for civilians. She then presented seven questions which were adopted in a motion to be presented to the Mayor and the Council. The questions are:
>
> 1. Is there any reason why the officers sworn to enforce the laws of the city and county should wait for action by private citizens to put an end to unlawful conditions which the officers know exist?
>
> 2. Would not the enforcement of the law eliminate the vicious conditions complained of?
>
> 3. When was the rank and file of the police and detective forces furnished with a list of the out of bounds places?
>
> 4. The authorities realize that only by taking direct action will the conditions be eliminated?
>
> 5. Do the authorities know the real owners and operators of the places of public entertainment which are engaged in unlawful and immoral practices?
>
> 6. Does not the law hold people who erect, condone, maintain use or occupy, lease or re-lease any building or place for the purposes of lewdness, assignation or prostitution, guilty of maintaining a nuisance?
>
> 7. Has the fact that the owners of the premises could be reached with a demand that they endeavor to clean up the existing conditions on their respective premises been considered by the authorities?

This list concluded the meeting with a thunderous applause. The groups represented at the meeting included the American Association of University Women, the Charleston Business and Professional Women's Club, the Women's Council for the Common Good, the Junior League, the Service Clubs Council, the Council of Catholic Women, the American Legion and Auxiliary, the Parent-Teacher Association, the Chamber of Commerce, the National Council of Jewish Women, and the Kiwanis Club, among others.

Harriet's newspaper clippings follow the progress of race relations both locally and nationally. She and Albert were supportive of the rights of Black citizens and progressive goals for integration. Associated work for health clinics that would be open to Black residents was a cause they supported, along with improved educational goals and sanitary living conditions. An indication of the struggles in Charleston included a 1942 clipping in her files reading, "The City of Charleston last year led by a wide margin all other cities in South Carolina in the number of robberies and aggravated assault cases known to police."

While Harriet was extremely involved in issues for the public good during the Depression, her work on behalf of the war effort was even more pronounced.

In a radio program in 1942 she shared:

The Civilian Defense Office has been going at top speed since December 7th. Sixty-Five hundred citizens of Charleston are hard at work under the defense set-up, and their services are of incalculable value to the city. A comprehensive knowledge of what the people of Charleston have done for their own defense should fill us all with pride. Any disaster that may come now will at least be minimized. We still want more workers however…

Come and register at Civilian Defense, 56 Wentworth Street, and see how your individual service can help the war effort. The activities in which men and women can work are Air Raid Wardens, Airplane Spotters, telephonists in the control room, and fire watchers. The men only services are Auxiliary Police, Auxiliary Firemen, and there is a great need for stretcher bearers for the casualty stations. Women are wanted for that most vital of services, the Filter Center. They can also work in many of the Red Cross activities, or for the U.S.O., or they may take the important and satisfying course as Nurses' Aid and give their hours of service in hospitals. The Rationing Board wants hours and days of service from Women.

Harriet was tireless in her work and that included the collection of materials such as aluminum that were needed for the war effort. In an April 8, 1942, letter from then-governor Jefferies, he wrote, "This is written to express my appreciation to you personally for the fine work that you are doing, and I shall be grateful if you will express these sentiments to all those who are serving under you in this splendid effort. I am especially appreciative of the fact that the whole civilian defense program has been set up without any thought of politics and we must keep politics entirely out of our efforts to win the war." Interesting to note, Harriet's daughter Serena was involved in the encryption of messages intercepted by American intelligence during the war.

Glancing Back, Steering Forward

Not magnitude, not lavishness,

But Form—the Site ;

Not innovating wilfulness,

But reverence for the Archetype.

(HERMAN MELVILLE, "Greek Architecture," 1891)

Albert Simons led the way in creating a planning department and planning board for the City of Charleston. A newspaper article from the 1970s called him the "Father of Planning" for Charleston County.[3]

Another article noted that he had created and served on the city's planning board since 1953, having worked toward the creation of the board since the mid-1940s. It continued, saying Simons "possesses the vision for the necessity and importance of good planning for both the immediate and future benefits of Charleston County and is at all times dedicated to serving in the best interests of all citizens of our county."[4]

The postwar period was a surprisingly busy time for the firm of Simons & Lapham in the form of Jack Mitchell, Jim Small, and Dennis Donahue. All of them had their names on the firm at some time, as did Sandy Logan for twelve years. The firm's work in these years is often considered a time of "quiet work" that fit in with the existing cityscape and appeared like it had always been there. One exception was the airport's design, but it was kept bare and simple more for budgetary reasons than not. What follows are some examples of the many projects that the firm completed in this era.

Simons's design work was always well-ordered, with quiet inventions that were necessary for the given site and conditions. An example of this is his design for the Fellowship Hall for St. Andrew's Lutheran Church in downtown Charleston. It has served the community for many years and with a somewhat humble symmetrical brick building that belies its hefty size and allows the historic white stuccoed church beside it to have prominence. On the interior it is deftly designed to be nicely detailed without being overwhelming for its intended uses.

Simons emphasized the importance to maintain some balance between beauty and utility in a 1952 letter to John Mead Howells:

Dear John,

Your account of the generosity of the New York Architects to Frank Lloyd Wright, and of his subsequent wasting of his substance in riotous living, only confirms the well established record. He is a completely amoral person. Perhaps Richard Wagner's music is no better, or no worse, because of his disregard for the basic laws of society, and the same might apply to the dancing of Isadora Duncan, but an Architect cannot be so irresponsible.

**St. Matthew's Lutheran Church Fellowship hall, Gothic-revival addition.
Photo by the author.**

Today we seem to lack any generally accepted standards of criticism
in the field of architecture. Certain august pundits like Lewis Mumford,
for example, base their judgments entirely on social usefulness; others
again regard any effort to attain beauty or emotional appeal as quite
disreputable. Of course, I realize that a return to Victorian romanticism
and sentimentality is neither likely nor desirable, but I would welcome a
somewhat more sympathetic understanding of the ever-present human
desire for subtlety and grandeur.

Simons's ambivalence about Modernism, and the constant pull that
he felt between looking back and looking forward, embodied how many
Charlestonians viewed their city. It was a city that venerated its past,
including its historic buildings, but also very much desired a place in
the modern world. Simons, therefore, was the perfect architect to help
shape the city's built environment as it developed in the postwar years.
And his impact was profound. His designs, and those of his firm, were
ubiquitous within Charleston. An article from November 22, 1973, sug-
gests the extent of his impact:

**O. T. Wallace building, ca. 1980, designed by Simons for
the County of Charleston.**

In the North Atlantic Wharf offices of the architectural firm of Simons,
Mitchell, Small, and Donahue there is a large map of the City of
Charleston with the neighborhoods south of Calhoun Street well
covered with tiny colored pins.

The pins represent projects completed by the two original partners of
the firm, Albert Simons and the late Samuel Lapham, and a substantial
majority of these projects were restorations on Charleston's important
dwellings, churches and public buildings.

According to Simons, who still remains active at his drafting table
at the age of 83, no one has had time to place any new pins in the map
since World War II or to replace many of the old ones as they fell off. He
reports that if the practice had been kept up for the last 30 years, the map
would be so studded with pins that it would be difficult to tell one block
from another for the lower peninsula.

This unusual career in period restoration over nearly a 60-year span
received at least partial recognition Wednesday with the unveiling of
a plaque for Simons at the Fireproof Building (which he had recently
restored)...

When asked about the number of anonymous designs he had completed over the years Simons didn't feel he could give a close count. "I know it has been a steady job but I couldn't guess how many drawings I've had to correct," he said. "Unfortunately for those of us who must pass on these matters, you can't tell a person what is good design," he said. "You have to show him a drawing and the staff has never existed to do this work."

Simons himself noted the dramatic changes that had come to the city, and the constant vigilance necessary to maintain its historic character. He shared his view in a 1974 letter to Abby Howells:

> Charleston has now become a tourist attraction the year round and houses are being kept in a state of repair and landscaping as never before. On the other hand our Board of Architectural Review has to wage a constant battle to prevent real estate adventures from destroying handsome old buildings to replace them with commonplace but more profitable structures. As the schools of Architecture throughout the country seem to pay little attention to traditional American Architecture and few of the architects now in their most productive years are unwilling or unable to design new buildings in harmony with their older neighbors. This is no doubt has always been so but the abandonment of classic principles makes the absence of harmony all the more offensive. No doubt these are the sentiments of an old man who has always held deep personal affection for his city.

Man of His Time, Architect for His Place

In an information request form for an honorary listing in a publication, Simons (at age 59) responded to their questions as follows:

QUESTION: What persons or influence have been most influential in your career? Why?

RESPONSE: My wife, Harriet Porcher Simons, because of her faith in me under all circumstances.

Joseph Aiken Simons, my brother, because of his aid and interest in my professional education.

The American Institute of Architecture because of its ideals and standards.

QUESTION: Please name, in the order of choice, the five persons whom you regard as having been most influential in the development of the United States.

RESPONSE: Thomas Jefferson for his basic ideas of Democracy;

John Marshall for the interpretation of the constitution;

Eli Whitney for inventing mass production;

George Washington for the eradication of epidemic disease;

Eugene V. Debs for defending the rights of labor.

QUESTION: Please name, in order of choice, the five greatest living Americans.

RESPONSE: Dwight D. Eisenhower—a military genius and integrity;

Bernard Baruch for wisdom and patriotism;

Robert Oppenheimer for scientific invention;

Robert Taft for political courage and integrity;

Thomas Parran for social courage and humanity.

These responses give a telling reflection on some of Albert's predilections. Baruch was living near Charleston at that time, and certainly Oppenheimer had a central role to play in the new nuclear-powered age.

It is interesting to note that Albert didn't mention any architects in his responses (he includes Jefferson for other reasons), but that is consistent with his other statements about the dearth of architects he considered great. Instead Simons called for discretion in the use of historical models for current architectural designs. "Today we are heirs of the ages and have access to all styles, but we should strive to use them with discretion and only when they accord with the character and purpose of the building; the architecture of history." That sense of conservatism, and predilection for preservation, despite a willingness to embrace the modern, would continue to define Simons's career into his later years.

Writing to the president of the College of Charleston in 1970 he noted the college's special role as the steward of several historic buildings and also repeated his belief, consistent with that pursued throughout his life, that professional planning led by a group of experts should help to guide the process. By engaging in this planning process, Simons promised that the college could derive the many benefits from its historic assets while simultaneously moving forward into the modern age.

Great niche at Randolph Hall, College of Charleston. This new colossal classical urban niche was designed by Simons in 1973 and coincided with the boom in new campus buildings.

As you know, the College of Charleston shares with many persons and organizations in the community a vital interest in the preservation of buildings of historical and architectural interest. The Bishop Smith House, the Lesesne House (Horizon House) and the buildings on the new College mall are recent examples of the College's contribution to the preservation of significant buildings.

The College is now about to enter a new phase of its 200 year history, a phase in which its growth will be far more rapid than any experienced in the past. During this period, the College must pay special attention to its role in area preservation to maintain its unique spirit and to emphasize its proud heritage.

To help guide the College in this matter, we are establishing a special Advisory Committee on Area Preservation. I am asking several persons whose contributions mark them as the community's leaders in the preservation field to volunteer their time to serve on this committee. On behalf of the College, I urge you to join us in this important work. (A list of community leaders who have been asked to serve is enclosed).

The Advisory Committee on Area Preservation would assist the College in recognizing buildings in the area and advise it on methods of preservation and on adaptive use of historic buildings in its plans. We also hope the committee will offer suggestions to the Board of Trustees on property purchases and on the design of new buildings.[5]

In a letter of May 11, 1971, to College of Charleston President Ted Stern, Simons reiterated his guiding ethos that the historic and the modern could coexist:

Thus, your building plans, your concern for preservation, your quite obvious enthusiasm for historic values were all quite refreshing to me. Of course, a college must grow, new buildings and facilities are required. And if the school is located in an urban area, where space is limited, the choices for location are also limited. But, I think it is possible to meet the demands of the present, build for the future, and retain the values of the past at the same time. No doubt, a bit more thought and planning are required, but it can be done. And, the values are beyond price. Colleges and universities are repositories, the custodians of our heritage and culture, and should implant a sense of continuity if nothing else. The alert and sensitive preservation of the past, not as relics, but as the setting for present activities, can be an education in itself.

A Legacy for All Seasons

Architect Sandy Logan recalled looking out the window from his drafting board seeing a terrible sight—Albert Simons looked both ways before stepping off the curb into the street, but a van came speeding by and the large side view mirror hit Albert hard. He struggled and suffered mightily after that collision, finally passing away three years later on May 23, 1980.

Simons's contributions to the fields of architecture, preservation, planning, art, and education transcend all conceivable potential limits. The AIA that he led is thriving and active today (see Appendix A—Simons's service to the AIA). The classical and traditional architecture he espoused has experienced a resurgence, as he said it would. In addition to practitioners of that mode of design, there is a New York–based group, the Institute for Classical Architecture and Art, that has chapters nationwide, and the Prince of Wales Institute in England teaches traditional architecture and crafts. As mentioned, he established the arts in the College with his courses starting in 1924 that is now a thriving School of the Arts. In addition to the Program in Historic Preservation and Community Planning in the Department of Art & Architectural History at the School of the Arts there is also a relatively new school called the American College for the Building Arts that is housed in Charleston. And an excellent graduate program in Historic Preservation jointly exists with the College of Charleston and Clemson University.

His buildings and many architectural alterations grace the Lowcountry, not only downtown but also in new and restored plantation-type houses and churches. There are now more than 800 historic districts in the United States, many modeled on the first one that Albert helped start in Charleston. There exist even more boards of architectural review, but few with such an effective member as Albert Simons was in Charleston, where he served on the BAR for forty-three years. In addition, he spent decades on the Regional Planning commission board. Ever the champion of comprehensive planning, his legacy lives on, though many challenges remain for Charleston and, indeed, the world. Expanding populations and looming environmental disaster demand more coordination now than ever before, yet many remain reluctant to embrace the need for such coordinated planning.

Nonetheless, the School of the Arts at the College of Charleston is thriving and has certainly transcended all expectations in the fields of art, music, theater, dance, and art history (in addition to the programs mentioned earlier). The books Simons created, with his beautiful drawings and informational texts, still are in print, and the survey efforts that culminated in the publication of *This Is Charleston* continue to guide preservation efforts in the city.

Upon his death in 1980, a newspaper column entitled "Albert Simons, A Gentleman" by Jack Leland in the Evening Post (Charleston), read:

> When he died here Saturday at almost 90 years of age he left behind
> a history of service to his community, state and nation that would be

ALBERT SIMONS
...ATION OF YEARS OF DEDICATIO
THE FINE ARTS

Bronze bas-relief of Simons by Willard Hirsch of Charleston.

difficult, if not impossible, to emulate today, a history that included military service in World Wars I and II—the latter when he was past 50, an age usually considered too great for civilian soldiers. He had practiced architecture here for 57 years and, while he left memorials of his work in brick, wood and stone, perhaps the greatest epitaph is written in the hundreds of buildings that were saved from destruction by actions in which he had a part.

...But Simons was not a "specialist," as so many modern professional men have become. He was truly a man for all seasons, a student throughout his life of the fine arts and their place in the lives of the well educated and the world in general....

Withal, Albert Simons was a gentle gentleman, with the courtesy and charm so inherent in the Old School and yet aware of the tremendously vital changes that were apparent all around him. He was truly a man of and in the world and his like will not come our way again.

Albert Simons at work at his drafting table well into his advanced years.
Courtesy Charleston Historical Society.

Albert Simons was intensely aware, as few others were, that there was a mind-bending set of changes around him. One can only imagine the impact on Simons of the Lunar Landing and the first stirrings of computers for myriad uses that began to be more common in the 1970s. His classical education and nineteenth-century beginnings made the furious technological advancements of the twentieth century extraordinary to him—a true transcendence of seemingly secure limits to change. He thought a lot about these things as he plowed ahead with his own classically derived designs while being aware of the technocratic ethos that was bearing down on architects of his vintage. He was cognizant as well of the ascendant preservation movement, launched as it was by such pioneers as Jacqueline Kennedy Onassis, who marched down New York City's Fifth Avenue with Henry Hope Reed (founder of the organization Classical America) to save Grand Central Station after witnessing the destruction of the grand McKim, Mead & White designed Penn Station.

Albert was a polymath. His rigorous, disciplined work ethic could inspire today's architects to serve in organizations to exercise their expertise as he did. With Charleston as his muse, Albert wrote and taught and sang and designed; his wife Harriet was very involved in his work while being a statewide proponent for women's rights; and they raised four wonderful children. He could "walk with kings, nor lose the common touch," in the words of Kipling.[6] He looked at life as a professional, yet with a subtle sense of humor at the things life threw his way, like serving in the camouflage corps during World War I. Would that every city could have such a man of great talent and vision working for so long in his traditional design practice, his national leadership in historic preservation, his striving to create regional planning and in his civic service.

Charleston Renaissance Continues

> Simons helped with his designs, restorations and advocacy, to save much
> of the old city and to create a harmonious bridge to it in its modern
> buildings.
>
> (JAMES HUTCHISSON and HARLAN GREENE, *Renaissance in*
> *Charleston*)

In 1975 Joseph P. Riley was elected mayor of Charleston. At only thirty-three years of age, Riley was the youngest mayor in the city's history, and he ascended to his role just as Albert Simons was nearing the end of his long career. During his forty years in office Riley led a grand comeback for the city of Charleston. His support for the arts and architecture that Simons did so much to foster were key to Riley's ability to lead the city on its late twentieth-century rise. Remnants of the 1910s and 1920s renaissance remain, though perhaps less evident than they once were. One example is Riley's work to create the Spoleto arts festival, which has borne fruit and crowned Charleston once again as a world-renowned destination for the highest artistic and cultural standards for varieties of music, theater, dance, and art. More subtle, but likely more significant, is the city's continued drive to retain the historic character of its buildings and landscape while simultaneously entering the next modern age. As seen before, the ability to navigate and meld these desires has proven the key to Charleston's vitality. The city's preserved foundational energy is Simons's legacy.

One can imagine that Albert Simons would approve of what has transpired in the city since he left. And one can't imagine the current artistic revival without his quiet, steadfast insistence on saving the architectural fabric, buildings so graciously designed to fit within the existing character, and his widespread contributions to artistic work in his forever hometown, the Holy City.

ALBERT SIMONS'S SERVICE TO THE AMERICAN INSTITUTE OF ARCHITECTS

Albert Simons had a long-standing relationship with the American Institute of Architects (AIA). In the 1930s he agreed to join the board of directors of the national office of the AIA. During the Great Depression Simons was busier than ever at his office with New Deal projects as well as private commissions. Yet in the mid-to-late 1930s Simons agreed to create and deliver lectures on architecture on behalf of the AIA. He traveled to numerous small South Carolina colleges, but he especially put himself out to travel up the Atlantic coast to lecture at Duke University, the University of Virginia, Princeton University (his son Stoney was a student there at the time), the University of North Carolina at Chapel Hill, and the Massachusetts Institute of Technology. He lectured at other schools such as Clemson, Georgia Tech, Virginia Tech, and locally at the Citadel. A newspaper reported on his Citadel lecture with attention given to his comment that there is not a completely adequate city anywhere.

In his first year of lecturing for the AIA, Simons focused on city plans through time, leading up to the then emerging interest in city planning. The next year his lectures focused on the history of American architecture, and after that he focused on Renaissance art and architecture. In 1938 his circuit homed in on Michelangelo's art and architecture. Lantern slides for his city history lecture included:

A plan of Babylon paired with the Ishtar Gate; ancient Athens paired with a view of the Acropolis; Roman forums; Carcassonne; a plan of Peiping paired with a view of the Forbidden City; the Alhambra; Piazza San Marco in Venice; St. Peter's and the Piazza Campidoglio; the Piazza del Popolo in Rome; Versailles and Paris; Wren's plans and St Paul's Cathedral; Washington, DC; the University of Virginia; the 1893 world's fair in Chicago; and Philadelphia. Some twentieth-century plans were shown of Forest Hills on Long Island in New York; Tyrone, NM; Radburn,

NJ; Letchworth, England; Canberra, Australia; and the government center in New Delhi.

In a 1937 letter to his friend William Emerson, dean of the architecture school at MIT, Albert Simons thanked Emerson for inviting himself and Harriet to the AIA convention in Boston:

> The Boston Convention has been a memorable experience and has inspired in us an affection for Boston which modernists would decry as sentimental, but which I believe is none-the-less sincere. I think our literary critics have long given us a misconception of the culture which centers about the hub; this has been a picture of "plain living and high thinking," which, while undoubtedly admirable, has always been a little forbidding for those of us of less strenuous mortal fiber. I feel that I have brought back an impression in which this Spartan background has been overlaid by a mellow and glamorous magnificence exemplified by the portraits of Gilbert Stuart and of Copely, the Bulfinch houses, the Symphony Orchestra and in Mr. Shepley's new buildings at Harvard, to mention only a few of the things which seem typical of much else of the same high quality. How does all this splendor stem from a background of austerity? Is it that a certain fastidiousness of mind finds its expression in one generation in the consideration of ethical problems and in the next turns more happily to aesthetic appreciation and creation? Though with each generation both ethical and aesthetic standards seem to shift and to be transformed, yet I believe that there is a certain residuum of wisdom and beauty which may be garnered for all time in those places where life has been stable and men have been thoughtful.
>
> With these ideas shaping themselves in my mind I did not find myself very sympathetic at Princeton to those strident protagonists of a "Brave New World" like George Howe nor to a champion of Medievalism like Mr. Klauder. Our language of today is not a synthetic Esperanto, nor is it the archaic speech of the Tudors. Whether we desire it or not, our architecture of today is inherently contemporary and it seems to be only a question whether it is to be so gracefully and decorously or with self-consciousness and vulgarity. I felt that some of those glib speakers in criticizing architectural education knew little of the sort of education provided today and were denouncing the limitations of education they had received thirty years ago. I felt that under the circumstances that your good nature and courtesy in conducting such a meeting had been subjected to an unnecessary strain and hoped that should I ever find myself in such a position, I would have the self-control and the wit to carry it off half as well.

While he is circumspect about his ambiguous-at-best view of modern architecture and art, he does write to George Forsythe at Princeton telling him that his work in Angres, France, has uncovered a complete history of classical and medieval architecture there; but, at the same time, in the next line he shares:

> In the hope of amusing so good an antiquarian, I am sending to you under separate cover the catalogue of the Guggenheim non-objective art exhibit held here last year; also of the Kress Italian exhibit. If you can't stand these you might pass them on to Dr. Panofsky (Irwin Panofsky was a famous Medieval scholar). I feel sure that he will produce at least one bon mot on each one.

Simons also gave popular public lectures about Charleston in the late 1940s and the early 1950s. An example was a lecture on improving the three entrance portals into the city, which were all plagued by derelict housing and "a mass of shacks, hot dog stands and filling stations." He used examples from the history of city form through time to make his point. He emphasized the need for good planning and zoning to improve the first impressions that the gateways provide visitors and residents alike.

COMMISSIONED WORK OF SIMONS AND LAPHAM

Known commissions of Simons & Lapham (partial list containing ready information). Listed by location (from the thesis of Ernest Blevins on his grandfather Samuel Lapham, completed at the Savannah College of Art and Design. Reprinted with permission.).

Georgia

Savannah, Chatham County

Whitfield Memorial Chapel Bethesda (1925), 9520 Ferguson Avenue

Christ Church (remodeling), Abercorn Street

North Carolina

Reidsville, Rockingham County

W. H. Pipkin Residence (1937), 633 South Main Street, Near Wilmington, Brunswick County

Remodeling of Section Base #2 (1941), Fort Caswell Naval Station, Southport

South Carolina

Aiken County, Aiken

St. Thaddeus Church (1926), 125 Pendleton Street, SW

Beaufort County

Twickenham Plantation (restoration) (1928), S. C. Secondary Road 33

Bonny Hall Plantation (additions) (1935), S. C. Secondary Road 33 (River Road)

Edgar W. Fripp's "Seaside Plantation," S. C. State Road 77

Laurel Springs Plantation (Extension), U. S. Highway 17, Beaufort

Beaufort County, City of Beaufort

St. Helena's Church Steeple (1940), 150 Church Street

Mather School Coleman Hall, 291 Rebault Street

Beaufort County, Parris Island Marine Base

Charlesfort Monument (1926), Parris Island

Main Barracks (1938), Parris Island

Rifle Range Barracks (1938), Parris Island

Mess Hall (1940), Parris Island

Post Exchange and Post Office Building (1941), Parris Island

Marine Corps Bakery (1941), Parris Island

Water Transportation Building (1942), Parris Island

War Memorial Building (1951), Parris Island

Berkeley County, South Carolina

Halidon Hill Plantation, Cooper River

The Oaks, Near Goose Creek

Oakland Plantation, Near St. Stephens

Oakly Plantation (ca. 1930), Near Oakley

Ophir Plantation, Near Pinopolis

Berkeley County, Yeamans Hall Plantation, Hanahan

Yeamans Hall Club and Grounds (1927–1930)

Simons designed 13 of the houses at Yeamans Hall

The Brewster Cottage, Yeamans Hall

The Colt Cottage, Yeamans Hall

The Day Cottage, Yeamans Hall

The Floyd-Jones Cottage, Yeamans Hall

The Griggs Cottage, Yeamans Hall

The McFadden Cottage, Yeamans Hall

The Pierrepont Cottage, Yeamans Hall

The Robertson Cottage, Yeamans Hall

The Thorne Cottage, Yeamans Hall

The Wales Cottage, Yeamans Hall

The Wiggins Cottage, Yeamans Hall

The Wilcox Cottage, Yeamans Hall

(Other architects involved in designing cottages at Yeamans Hall included James Gamble Rogers, Grosvenor Atterbury, Laurence Hall Fowler, and also Sandy Logan who had previously worked for Albert Simons.)

Camden County, Camden

Bloomsbury (Restoration) (1931) 1707 Lyttleton Street

Grace Church Parish House (1932) 1315 Lyttleton Street

Charleston County

Rice Hope Plantation Cooper River near Moncks Corner

(Extension) (1931)

The Wedge Plantation (Restoration) (ca. 1929) Santee River near McClellanville

Prospect Hill Near Jacksonboro

Willtown Bluff Near Jacksonboro

Tibwin Plantation Near McClellanville

Rosebank Plantation John's Island

Anderson Memorial Flagpole (1931) Fort Sumter

City of Charleston

Porter Military Academy Dormitory Repairs (1927) Ashley Avenue

Standard Oil Service Station (1929) 305 Ashley Avenue

Wraggsborough Project (1939–1940) America/South/Draker/Chapel Streets

St. Johanne's Sunday School Building (1927) 43 Anson Street

Memminger Elementary School (1953) 20 Beaufain Street

Memminger Auditorium (1938) 50 Beaufain Street

Robert mills Manor I and II (1935–37) Beaufain/Logan/Magazine

Carolina Savings Bank (renovation) 1 Broad Street

SC National Bank Extension (1928) 16 Broad at State Street

American Mutual Fire Insurance Company 19 Broad Street

American Mutual F. I. A. C. 100 Broad Street

Standard Oil Service Station (1929) 102 Cannon Street

The Tire Company (1927) 149 Cannon Street

Ansonborough Projects (1940) (gone) End of Calhoun Street

Standard Oil Station (1930) 248 Calhoun Street

Thomas Memorial Infirmary (1920) 288–300 Calhoun Street

County Tuberculosis Hospital (1920) Calhoun Street

West Point Mill (adaptive reuse 1941) Calhoun Street

Pink House (restoration) (1931) 17 Chalmers Street

Josephine Pinckney (remodeling, 1931) 36 Chalmers Street

Murray Vocational School Auto Shop Annex 3 Chisholm Street

Gord Residence (Remodeling) (1940) 19 Church Street

Whitman Residence (restoration) (1930) 59 Church Street

Heyward-Washington House (1931) 87 Church Street

Dock Street Theater (Restoration) (1935–38) 135 Church Street

Chancel, St. Phillip's Church (1920) Church Street

Parish House Addition,

St. Phillips Episcopal Church (1927) Church Street

Publishing Plant, Charleston News and Courier 134 Columbus Street

College of Charleston Student Activities Building (1939) 24 George
    Street

West Wing (chemistry), Randolph Hall, College of Charleston (1930) 66
    George Street

College of Charleston Heating Plant (1927) 66 George Street

Craig Dormitory and Cafeteria (1962) George Street

Robert Smalls Library (1972) 66 George Street

"Cougar Mall," College of Charleston Campus 66 George Street

Julius Visanska Residence (ca. 1930) 19 East Battery

Hanahan Residence (Restoration) (1925) 43 East Battery

Omar Temple (Restoration) (1925) 40 East Bay Street

Fort Sumter Chevrolet Company (1954) East Bay Street

Nicholas G. Roosevelt Residence (1930 remodeling) 71 East Bay Street

Martin Residence (restoration) (1936) 89 East Bay

Standard Oil Service Station (1931) 102 East Bay

East Bay Elementary (1954) upper East Bay

Carolina Mutual Insurance 10 Elliott Street

Gadsden Garden Homes (1940's) Near the Citadel

Samuel Lapham Residence (addition) 4 Greenhill Street

Wyman Residence (1938) 20 Greenhill Street

Residence (1937) 311 Grove Street

Lowndes Grove Plantation (remodel) (1939) 266 St. Margaret Street

K. K. B. E. Tabernacle 90 Hassell Street

Residence (restoration) 54 Hasell Street

Medical College Library & Dept. of Pathology (1930) 86 Jonathan Lucas Street

Masonic Temple (remodel) (1922) King & Wentworth Streets

Robert Wilson Residence 43 King Street

Guest House (rear addition) (1937) 46 King Street

Drotter Residence (1928) 51 King Street

Gate of the Unitarian Churchyard (1922) 163 King Street

Jack Krawcheck Store (remodel) (1946) 311 King Street

St. Matthew's Lutheran Church Parish House (1932) 405 King Street

St. Matthew's Lutheran Steeple and Sanctuary (restoration) (1965–66) 405 King Street

Branch of People's National Bank (1927) 544 King Street

Standard Oil Service Station (1929) 669 King Street

Rivers Junior High School (1928) 1000 King Street

Residence (renovation) 12 Lamboll Street

Schuyler L. Parsons Residence 18 Lamboll

Mrs. A. E. Geer Residence 1 Legare Street

Hagood Residence (Remodeling) 18 Legare Street

Theodore Simons Jr. Residence (1921) 17 Lenwood Street

Cavalry Church, Fellowship Hall and Reverend's House Complex Percy Street

Middleton Residence (1928) 2 Lowndes Street

Westminister Presbyterian Church (1927) 26 Maverick

Standard Oil Service Station (1931) 108 Meeting Street

The Tire Company 256 Meeting Street

Masonic Temple Renovation (post–WWII) 287 Meeting at George

Standard Oil Service Station (1931) 102 East Bay Street

Ashley Ice Cream, Inc. Garage 574–576 Meeting Street

Meeting Street Manor (1937) Meeting/Harris/Johnson/Nassau

Cooper River Courts (1937) Meeting/Harris/Johnson/Nassau

Standard Oil Service Station (1929) 584 Meeting Street

H. K. Koebig Residence 28 Murray Blvd

R. B. Rhett Residence 46 Murray Blvd

Middleton Residence (1929) 48 Murray Blvd

St. Michael's Church Parish House/ 5 St. Michael's Alley

main building remodeling (1925)

Archer School (1935) Nassau Street

Archer School Additions (1936) Nassau Street

Addition to Burke High School (1923) President Street

Westminster Presbyterian Parish Home (1927) Rutledge Avenue

Durham Life Insurance Company (1966) 144 Rutledge Street

Lowndes Grove Renovations 260 St. Margaret's Street

Standard Oil Station (1930) 73 Saint Philip's Street

Sumter Guards' Armory

Remodeling and addition (1926) 80½ Society Street

Robertson Residence (remodeling) (1939) 39 South Battery

Judge Joseph Aiken Residence 53 South Battery

L. DeB. McCrady Residence (1937) 74 South Battery

Episcopal Residence (1933) 129 South Battery

Albert Simons Residence 84 South Battery

E. H. Jefford's Residence (1921) 100 South Bay

Taft Residence (1935) 135 South Bay

Standard Oil Station (1929) 56 State Street

St. Andrew's Lutheran Parish House (1931) 37–43 Wentworth St.

Scottish Rite Cathedral (Silas Rogers Mansion [1920 on])

Renovations and changes 149 Wentworth Street

Joseph E. Jenkins Residence (1922) Charleston

Peyton J. Clark Residence Charleston

Charleston, Charleston Naval Yard

Cafeteria (1939)

Riggers and Laborer's Shop

Chapel (1942)

Tillman Homes (1940)

Charleston County, Edisto, and Edisto River Vicinity

Seabrook House (Restoration) (1929)

Seabrook House, Garage and servants' Quarters (new) (1931)

Quarters (new) (1931)

Prospect Hill Plantation, Dog Kennel's and Keeper's House

Frank L. Hutten (1929) Laurel Hill Rd.

Grove Plantaton (Restoration) (1929) Nr. Jacksonboro

Willtown Bluff Plantation (1931)

Smith Plantation (renovation) (1929)

Folly Beach, Charleston County, South Carolina

B. P. O. Elks' Summer Home

James Island, Charleston County, South Carolina

Hancock Residence 9 Belvedere Lane

Henneniger Residence Country Club vicinity

Van Buren Residence 4 Country Club Road

Fenwick Hall (restoration) (1934) River Road

St. James Episcopal Church (1965) Maybank Highway

North Charleston, Charleston County, South Carolina

North Charleston High School 1087 Montagu

First National Bank Branch 3300 Rivers Ave.

Municipal Airport Terminal Building (Simons) Aviation Avenue

Baptist College (now Charleston Southern) U.S. Hwy 78

(Local for Perry Dean Hepburn & Stewart of Boston, MA)

Sullivan's Island, Charleston County, South Carolina

"What a Site" (Lapham family beachhouse), Station 22½

Officer's Club (Jasper Hall) (1933) 1735 Atlantic Avenue

Colleton County

Hope Plantation (1928) SC State Road 30

Poco Sabo Plantation (new) (1934) SC Secondary Road 26

Combahee (aka Hamberg) remodeled (1942) SC State Road 66

White Hall Plantation (1925) SC Secondary Rd 119

Longview Plantation

Laurel Spring Plantation (1940) US Hwy 17 nr. Green Pond

Darlington County, City of Hartsville

Charles W. Coker Residence (1941) Hartsville, SC

Georgetown County

Prince George Winyah Parish House (1925) SC Secondary Road 119

Litchfield Plantation Restoration (1926) Near Georgetown

Windsor Plantation (Paul Mills residence) (new, 1938) Georgetown

Exchange Plantation btwn Georgetown and Lake City

J. H. Carter Residence Lake City, SC

Jasper County

Chelsea Plantation (Marshall Field III) off US Hwy 278

Residence (new) (1938) Near Ridgeland

Okeetee Club (1959) US Hwy 17 Switzerland, SC

Huspah Plantation

Simons & Lapham remodeling/restoration projects in Charleston
  (based on handwritten notes by Samuel Lapham in a copy of *This is
  Charleston* from 1944; some overlap with entries above).

St. John's Lutheran Church 10 Archdale Street

South Carolina National Bank 16 Broad Street

Simons & Lapham Building (gone) 100 Broad Street

Orphan House (gone) 160 Calhoun Street

Orphan House Chapel (gone) 13 Vanderhorst Street

Calvery Episcopal Church (gone) 71 Beaufain Street

West Point Mill Calhoun Street (west)

The Pink House 17 Chalmers Street

    36 Chalmers Street

    19 Church Street

    59 Church Street

    79 Church Street

    87 Church Street

    90 Church Street

Dock Street Theater Church Street

St. Phillip's Episcopal Church Street

Powder Magazine Cumberland Street

Shriners at East Battery 40 East Bay Street

    43 East Bay

    51 East Bay

    71 East Bay

    89 East Bay

    103 East Bay

Marine Hospital 20 Franklin Street

Randolph Hall, College of Charleston 66 George Street

Old Library, College of Charleston 66 George Street

Samuel Axon House (Lapham Residence) 4 Greenhill Street

Lowndes Grove Plantation House Grove Street (west end)

    54 Hasell Street

Beth Elohim 74 Hasell Street

    19 King Street

    313 King Street

    405 King Street

    18 Legare Street

Wingate House 21 Legare Street

St. Andrew's Society Hall 72 Meeting Street

St. Michael's Church 80 Meeting Street

    281 Meeting Street (gone)

Joseph Manigault House 350 Meeting Street

Citadel Square Baptist Church Meeting Street

Charleston Free Library 94 Rutledge Street

    67 Smith Street

General William Washington House 8 South Battery

Magwood House 39 South Battery

Gibbs House 64 South Battery

Pettus House 68 South Battery

Former office of Simons & Lapham 7 State Street

Col. John Stuart House 106 Tradd Street 2 Water Street

St Andrew's Lutheran Church 43 Wentworth Street

Silas Rogers Mansion 149 Wentworth Street

NOTES

Introduction

1. The appellation "City by the Sea" is mentioned in a ca. 1898 publication called "Charleston, South Carolina: Its Advantages, Its Conditions, Its Prospects, A Brief History of the 'City By the Sea.'"

Chapter 1. From a Charleston Family

1. His siblings include Joseph Aiken Simons; Serena Aiken Simons; Thomas Grange Simons IV; Ellen Aiken Simons (1884–1886); William Lucas Simons; and Robert Bentham Simons II.
2. Simons family book in the South Carolina Historical Society (SCHC).
3. Severans, 134.

Chapter 2. My Lost Youth, 1890–1905

1. 26-46-6 of the Simons Papers, SCHS 7/31/47.
2. See *Charlestonians Abroad: The Politics of Taste in Antebellum Charleston* by Maurie McGuinness, Chapel Hill: University of North Carolina Press, 2005. The introduction notes on page 8 state that: "In 1774 the South Carolina Lowcountry was by far the wealthiest area in British North America. Economic Historians have estimated that in the Charleston District per free capita wealth was more than ten times greater than that of New England. By 1860, the Lowcountry still compared favorably to other regions with a per free capita wealth more than three times greater than most Northern cities." McGuinness footnotes the book *Shadow of a Dream* by Peter Coclanis that asserts "The per free capita wealth calculates wealth based on the free inhabitants. In 1860 Charleston's per free capita wealth was more than $2,200 (per capita nearly $800), while Massachusetts per capita wealth was just over $625, and in New York it was under $600."
3. Big storms hit the Lowcountry in 1911 and 1913 and destroyed most remaining rice fields.
4. Letter from Albert Simons to Abby Howells in the Simons papers, SCHS.

Chapter 3. College of Charleston, Penn, and Paris, 1906–1913

1. John Nolen, *New Towns for Old*, repr., University of Massachusetts Press, 2005.
2. SCHS 26-59-2.

3. Simons papers at the South Carolina Historical Society.

4. George S. Chappell, "Paris School Days: How the Student Lives and Works at the Ecole des Beaux Arts," *Architectural Record* (July 1910): 38.

5. Chappell, "Paris School Days," 38–39.

6. Typed paper in Albert Simons personal papers at the South Carolina Historical Society.

Chapter 4. Early Experience and a World War, 1914–1920

1. Harlen/ Wadell p. 117.

2. Harlen/Wadell chapter.

3. SCHS 26-46-3 and SCHS 26-46-2.

4. F. Melendez, ed., "Architects in Profile: Albert Simons, FAIA."

5. "John Mead Howells Dies: Authority on Architecture." *New York Herald Tribune.*

Chapter 5. When "Charleston" Was a Dance

1. Severans, *Charleston Antebellum.*

2. Mark Knowles, *The Wicked Waltz and Other Scandalous Dances: Outrage at Couple Dancing in the 19th and Early 20th Centuries.* (Jefferson, NC: McFarland, 2009), 137.

3. Saunders and McAden. *Alfred Hutty and the Charleston Renaissance,* 13.

4. Arnold and Hoffius, *The Life and Art of Alfred Hutty.*

5. Greene, *Mr. Skylar,* 134.

6. Hosmer, *Preservation Comes of Age,* 232.

7. Yuhl, *The Making of Historic Charleston.*

8. Harlan/Waddell, 121.

9. Ibid., 21.

10. While the history of the preservation movement in Charleston has been covered by many publications, the best source is still the two volume *Preservation Comes of Age* by Charles Hosmer as he communicated directly with Albert Simons to guide his account of the movement in Charleston. Other helpful sources include portions of *Historic Preservation for a Living City* by Robert Weyeneth, and Robert Weyeneth's chapter in *Giving Preservation a History,* edited by Randall Mason.

11. Hosmer, *Preservation Comes of Age,* 242.

12. Hosmer, 235—Alston Deas, interview by Charles Hosmer, 1972.

13. Albert Simons as quoted in Weyeneth.

14. Correspondence from Ehren Foley, October 8, 2020.

15. Information from Hosmer, 242–43.

16. Includes information from Hosmer, 245.

17. Hosmer, 238–39. Other members of the committee included Alston Deas, Frank Lessman (realtor), Burnet Rhett Maybank (alderman who was later the mayor and then a US senator), and R. S. MacElwee (commissioner of the Bureau of Port Development who pushed hard for a new ordinance and even drafted one of his own based on the early zoning experience of the cities of Cleveland, OH, and Norfolk, VA).

18. Hosmer, *Preservation Comes of Age,* 240.

19. Based on Hosmer.

20. Hosmer, *Preservation Comes of Age,* 240–41.

21. Correspondence between Simons and Emerson, Simons archives.

22. Waddell, *Charleston Architecture,* 116–17.

23. Yeamans Hall Club, Yeaman's Hall, Charleston, 1930, p. 2.

24. Hutchisson and Greene, *Renaissance in Charleston,* 79.

25. Gwen Shepherd Davis, "Charleston Etcher's Club and Early Charleston Printmakers" (master's thesis, University of South Carolina, 1982).

26. Yuhl, *Making of Historic Charleston,* 89–90. Amy Lowell was from the imagist school of American poetry; she passed in 1925 at age fifty-one.

27. Hutchisson and Greene, *Renaissance in Charleston,* 66.

28. Yuhl, *Making of Historic Charleston,* 92.

29. Ibid., 96.

30. Ibid.

31. SCHS.

32. Harlan Greene, "'Mr. Bennett's Amiable Desire': The Poetry Society of South Carolina and the Charleston Renaissance," in Hutchisson and Greene, *Renaissance in Charleston,* 72.

33. College of Charleston Special Collections, box 1, folder 2.

Chapter 6. Rescue from the Storm, 1931–1945

1. Yuhl, *Making of Historic Charleston,* 42.

2. Burnet Maybank, rededication speech for the Dock Street Theater, 1937.

3. Yuhl, *Making of Historic Charleston,* 37.

4. Ibid., 36.

5. Harriet Simons, preface to *Plantations of the Carolina Low Country,* 1938.

6. bridges, p. 301.

7. Suzannah Smith Miles, "Fenwick Hall Plantation," *Charleston Magazine* (April 2018).

8. Hosmer, *Preservation Comes of Age,* 261–62.

Chapter 7. Transcended Limits, 1946–1980

1. Herbert DeCosta Jr. (papers, Avery Research Center, College of Charleston).

2. Clipping from the *Evening Post* (Charleston) newspaper does not indicate the year of this meeting, but it appears to be from the late 1930s.

3. "Planning 'Father' Honored." *Evening Post* (Charleston), SCHS files.

4. Barbara Williams, "County Officials Honor Simons," Charleston newspaper, April 8, 1975.

5. Invited members: Mrs. Frances S. Edmunds, director, Historic Charleston Foundation; Mr. Peter Manigault, publisher, *Post and Courier (Charleston);* Mr. Albert Simons, architect, Simons, Lapham, Mitchell and Small; Mr. Theodore S. Stem, president, College of Charleston; Mr. Thomas L. Stevenson, president, Historic Charleston Foundation; and Mrs. Joseph R. Young, president, Preservation Society of Charleston.

6. Rudyard Kipling, "If–," *A Choice of Kipling's Verse* (New York: Charles Scribner's Sons, 1943).

BIBLIOGRAPHY

"Albert Simons, F.A.I.A." *South Carolina Magazine,* vol. 21, no. 12, December 1957, 20.

"Architecture in Profile: Albert Simons, AIA." "Review of Architecture: South Carolina," October 1961, 6–8, 24–25.

Arnold, Sara C., and Stephen G. Hoffius. *The Life and Work of Alfred Hutty: Woodstock to Charleston.* Columbia: University of South Carolina Press, 2012.

Bland, Sidney. *Preserving Charleston's Past, Shaping Its Future: The Life and Times of Susan Pringle Frost.* Columbia: University of South Carolina Press, 1999.

Board of Architectural Review minutes. Charleston, SC: City of Charleston Archives, 1931–1974.

Bruder, Stanley. *Visionaries and Planners.* New York: Oxford University Press, 1990.

Burghardt, Laura Ashley. "The Movement of Architectural Elements Within Charleston, SC." master's thesis, Clemson University/College of Charleston Graduate Program in Historic Preservation, 2009.

"Charleston Helps Revive Interest in American Architecture." *News and Courier* (Charleston, SC), December 25, 1938.

Dowling, Elizabeth. *American Classicist: Philip Tramwell Schutze.* New York: Rizzoli Publishers, 2001.

Drexler, Arthur. *The Architecture of the Ecole des Beaux-Arts.* Cambridge, MA: MIT Press, 1977.

Egbert, Donald Drew. *The Beaux-Arts Tradition in French Architecture.* Princeton, NJ: Princeton University Press, 1980.

Galligan, Edward. "Albert Simons: 'There's a Lot of Work Left.'" *News and Courier* (Charleston, SC), 11 September 1977, 3-E.

Greene, Harlan. *Mr. Skylark: John Bennett and the Charleston Renaissance.* Athens: University of Georgia Press, 2001.

Hare, James. "Exaggerated Reverence for the Past: The Challenge of Design Review in the Charleston Historic District." *Design and Historic Preservation: The Challenge of Compatibility.* Edited Ames, David, and Richard Wagner. Newark: University of Delaware Press, 2009, 43–60.

Hewitt, Mark. *Mott B. Schmidt.* New York: Rizzoli Publishers, 1991.

Hosmer, Charles. *Preservation Comes of Age: From Williamsburg to the National Trust, 1926–1949.* Charlottesville: University of Virginia Press, 1981.

Hutchisson, James. "Building on the Past: Architect Albert Simons Saved Charleston's Historical Legacies While Planning Its Future." *Charleston Magazine,* March 2007, 95.

Hutchisson, James, and Harlean Greene, eds. *Renaissance in Charleston: Art and Life in the Carolina Lowcountry, 1900–1940.* Athens: University of Georgia Press, 2003.

McGuinness, Maurie. *In Pursuit of Refinement: Charlestonians Abroad, 1740–1860.* Columbia: University of South Carolina Press, 1999.

Melendez, F. "Architects in Profile: Albert Simons, FAIA." Preservation Society of Charleston, *Preservation Progress,* no. 2 (1963): 4–5.

Muldrow, Ralph. "A Charleston Architect: Albert Simons." *Preservation Progress, The Journal of the Preservation Society of Charleston* (2013).

———. "Albert Simons: Southern Severity and Quiet Classicism in Charleston." *The Classicist,* no. 8 (2009): 28–33.

Phillips, Ted Ashton, Jr. *City of the Silent: The Charlestonians of Magnolia Cemetery.* Columbia: University of South Carolina Press, 2010.

"Planning Father Honored." *Charleston Evening Post* (SC), April 8, 1975.

Poston, Jonathan. *The Buildings of Charleston: A Guide to the City's Architecture.* Columbia: University of South Carolina Press, 1997.

Ravenel, Beatrice St. Julien. *Architects of Charleston.* Columbia: University of South Carolina Press, 1992.

Rogers, George. *Charleston in the Age of the Pinckneys.* Columbia: University of South Carolina Press, 1980.

Rosen, Robert. *A Short History of Charleston.* Columbia: University of South Carolina Press, 1999.

Saunders, Boyd, and Ann McAden. *Alfred Hutty and the Charleston Renaissance.* Orangeburg, SC: Sandlapper, 1990.

Severens, Kenneth. *Charleston: Antebellum Architecture and Civic Destiny.* Knoxville: University of Tennessee Press, 1988.

Severens, Kenneth. "Toward Preservation Before 1931: The Early Career of Albert Simons." *Preservation Progress,* Preservation Society of Charleston, (Spring 1993): 9.

Simons, Albert. *The Early Architecture of Charleston.* Columbia: University of South Carolina Press, 1990. First published 1927 by the American Institute of Architects (New York).

Stoney, Samuel, and Albert Simons. *Plantations of the Low Country.* Charleston: Carolina Art Association, 1938.

Strong, Ann L., and George Thomas. *The Book of the School. 100 Years: The Graduate School of Fine Arts of the University of Pennsylvania,* 1990.

Sully, Susan. *Charleston Style: Past and Present.* New York: Rizzoli, 1999.

Waddell, Gene. *Charleston Architecture: 1670–1860.* Charleston, SC: Wyrick, 2003.

Yuhl, Stephanie. *The Making of Historic Charleston: A Golden Haze of Memory.* Chapel Hill: University of North Carolina Press, 2005.

INDEX

Italicized page numbers refer to illustrations.